The Earth Is the Lord's

The Earth Is the Lord's

THE INNER WORLD OF THE JEW IN EASTERN EUROPE

BY

ABRAHAM JOSHUA HESCHEL

WITH WOOD ENGRAVINGS BY ILYA SCHOR

A JEWISH LIGHTS
Classic Reprint

JEWISH LIGHTS Publishing
Woodstock, Vermont

The Earth Is the Lord's:
      The Inner World of the Jew in Eastern Europe

A JEWISH LIGHTS Classic Reprint

Library of Congress Cataloging-in-Publication Data

Heschel, Abraham Joshua, 1907-1972.
The Earth Is the Lord's : the inner world of the Jew in Eastern
Europe / Abraham Joshua Heschel : with wood engravings by Ilya Schor.
            p.   cm.   —   (A Jewish Lights classic reprint)
Previously published: New York : Farrar, Straus, Giroux, 1949.

ISBN 1-879045-42-7 (trade pbk.)

1. Judaism—Europe, Eastern. 2. Spiritual life—Judaism. 3. Jewish way of life.
   4. apws—Europe, Eastern—Social life and customs. I. Title. II. Series.
            BM290.H47   1995   95-5380
            296'0947—dc20   CIP

First Paperback Edition
10 9 8 7 6 5 4 3 2

Manufactured in the United States of America

Published by Jewish Lights Publishing
A Division of LongHill Partners Inc.
P.O. Box 237
Sunset Farm Offices, Route 4
Woodstock, VT 05091
Tel: 802 457-4000   Fax: 802 457-4004

Contents

Preface

THE STORY ABOUT THE LIFE OF THE JEWS IN EASTERN EUROPE WHICH HAS COME TO AN END IN OUR DAYS IS WHAT I HAVE tried to tell in this essay. I have not talked about their books, their art or institutions, but about their daily life, about their habits and customs, about their attitudes toward the basic things in life, about the scale of values which directed their aspirations.

It is a story about an entire era in Jewish history, in which the attempt is made to portray the character of a people as reflected in its way of living throughout generations, in its loyalties and motivations, in its unique and enduring features. Viewed from a wide historical perspective, issues that loomed important in recent years were considered only in proportion to the total picture of the Ashkenazic period which extended over eight hundred years.[1]

My task was, not to explain, but to see, to discern and to depict. An investigation of the social, economic, and political factors which were effective during the period, and their impact upon the spirit of the people was not within the scope of this essay. It was likewise not my intention to dwell upon the various achievements of that period, such as the contributions to science and literature, to art and theology, the rise of the *Wissenschaft des Judentums*,[2] the revival of the Hebrew language, the modern Hebrew and Yiddish literatures, the development of the Yiddish language, Zionism, Jewish socialism, the establishment of new centers, the rebuilding of Israel, the various attempts to modernize Jewish life and to adapt it to changing conditions.

For how do we appraise the historic significance of a period? By what standards do we

[1] The East European period was a phase in the development of Ashkenazic Jewry, see page 24.
[2] Modern scientific research in Jewish history and literature.

8

measure culture? It is customary in the modern world to evaluate a period by its progress in general civilization, by the quality of the books, by the number of universities, by the artistic accomplishments, and by the scientific discoveries made therein. As Jews, with an old tradition for appraising and judging events and generations, we evaluate history by different criteria, namely, by how much refinement there is in the life of a people, by how much spiritual substance there is in its everyday existence. In our eyes, culture is the style of the life of a people. We gauge culture by the extent to which a whole people, not only individuals, live in accordance with the dictates of an eternal doctrine or strive for spiritual integrity; the extent to which inwardness, compassion, justice and holiness are to be found in the daily life of the masses.

The pattern of life of a people is more significant than the pattern of its art. What counts most is not expression, but existence itself. The key to the source of creativity lies in the will to cling to spirituality, to be close to the inexpressible, and not merely in the ability of expression. What is creative comes from responsive merging with the eternal in reality, not from an ambition to say something. To appraise adequately the East European period in Jewish history, I had to inquire into the life-feeling and life-style of the people. This led to the conclusion that in this period our people attained the highest degree of inwardness. I feel justified in saying that it was the golden period in Jewish history, in the history of the Jewish soul.

The Earth Is the Lord's

The Sigh

OST OF US SUCCUMB TO THE MAGNETIC PROPERTY OF THINGS AND EVALUATE EVENTS BY THEIR TANGIBLE RESULTS. We appreciate things that are displayed in the realm of Space. The truth, however, is that the genuinely precious is encountered in the realm of Time, rather than in Space. Monuments of bronze live by the grace of the memory of those who gaze at their form, while moments of the soul endure even when banished to the back of the mind. Feelings, thoughts, are our own, while possessions are alien and often treacherous to the self. To be is more essential than to have. Though we deal with things, we live in deeds.

Pagans exalt sacred things, the Prophets extol sacred deeds. The most precious object that has ever been on earth were the Two Tablets of stone which Moses received upon Mount Sinai: "The tablets were the work of God, and the writing was the writing of God, graven upon the tablets." [1] But when coming down the mount—the Two Tablets he had just received in his hands—Moses saw the people dance around the Golden Calf, he cast the Tablets out of his hands and broke them before their eyes.

The stone is broken, but the Words are alive. The replica Moses had subsequently made is gone too, but the Words did not die. They still knock at our gates as if begging to be engraved "on the Tablets of every heart." While others have carried their piety, fervor, faith into magnificent songs of architecture, our ancestors had neither the skill nor the material necessary to produce comparable structures. Phoenician craftsmen had to be brought to Jerusalem by Solomon the King to assist in erecting the Temple for the Lord. But there were Jews who knew how to lay bricks in the soul, to rear holiness made of simple deeds, of study and prayer, of care, of fear and love. They

[1] Exodus 32:16.

knew how to pattern and raise a pyramid that no one could see but God.

The Jews in Eastern Europe lived more in time than in space. It was as if their soul was always on the way, as if the secret of their heart had no affinity with things. It is rarely given to an artist to convey their spirit in color and line. A *niggun*, a tune flowing in search of its own unattainable end; a story in which the soul surprises the mind; a *knaitsh*, the subtle shading of a thought, or a fervent gesture, which puts a situation, as it were, in God's quotation marks, is perhaps more suggestive of their essence.

He was a unique type of man, the Jew in Eastern Europe, one whose habits and taste did not conform to classical standards of beauty, but who nevertheless was endowed with a wistful charm; one whose physiognomy was not like a passage in an open book—a static picture of uniform lines with a definite proportion of text and margin—but like a book whose pages are constantly turning.

That charm came from the inner richness of their being—from the polarity of reason and feeling, of joy and sorrow, from the mixture of intellectualism and mysticism which is often bewildering to analytical observers. Their spirit was not like the luster of a sedate pearl, softly shining in patience and tranquillity, but rather scintillating like a tremulous gleam of light, like the twinkle of cut gems.

To be gay, carefree, relaxed, was an art few of them ever learned. A Jewish child would be taught that life was too earnest to be wasted on play. Joy, when felt, was always for a serious reason, the trimming for a happy occasion, justified like a logical conclusion.

There were many who did not trust words, and their deepest thoughts would find expression in a sigh. Sorrow was their second soul, and the vocabulary of their heart consisted of one sound: "Oy!" And when there was more than the heart could say, their eyes would silently bear witness. It was, indeed, indicative of their state of mind that, generation after generation, some of their leaders had felt called upon to teach that cheerfulness was not a sin, but, on the contrary, the absence of it was.

There was restrained mourning in their enthusiasm, profound sadness in their joy. Their authentic chants are consistently in the minor key. The melodies which the wedding players intoned before the veiling ceremony would almost rend the soul of the bride. The *badhan*, the merry-maker, would paint in a wailing voice the suffering and hardship which life holds in store for every human being. Under the *hupah*—the bridal canopy—bride, mother, and grandmother would sob, and even a man who heard a piece of good news would usually burst into tears. But the Jews all sang: the student over the Talmud, the tailor while sewing a pair of trousers, the cobbler while mending tattered shoes, and the preacher while delivering a sermon.

T W O

"With All Thy Heart"

THEY DID NOT MAKE THE MISTAKE OF THINKING THAT THE GOOD IS ATTAINED UNWITTINGLY AND THAT HOURS HAVE merely to be lived in order to arrive at the goals of living. To communicate with the goal, one has to address himself to it. What is undirected, what is done at haphazard, goes astray.

They had disdain for the rough, for the coarse, and tried to lend an inward dignity to everything they did. Not only the extraordinary days, not only the Sabbath, even their weekdays had a form. Everything was fixed according to a pat-

18

tern. Nothing was casual, nothing was left to chance.

The dishes to be served on certain days, the manner of putting on or removing one's shoes, the stance of one's head when walking in the street—everything was keyed to a certain style. Every part of the liturgy, every prayer, every hymn, had its own tune; every detail its own physiognomy, each object its individual stamp. Even the landscape became Jewish. In the month of Elul[1] during the penitential season, the fish in the streams trembled; on *Lag ba-Omer*,[2] the scholar's festival in the spring, all the trees rejoiced. When a holiday came, even the horses and dogs felt it. And a crow perched on a branch looked from a distance "as though it were wearing a white prayer shawl, with dark blue stripes in front, and it sways and bends as it prays, and lowers its head in intense supplication."

But they also had sufficient vitality to constantly modify the accepted pattern. New customs were continually added to, and the old customs enriched by nuances. Unaltered forms and

[1] Approximately September, the month preceding the Days of Awe—New Year and the Day of Atonement. The month of Elul is devoted to inner preparation and self-examination in anticipation of the heavenly judgment on the Days of Awe.

[2] The thirty-third day of a counting of days that begins with the second day of Passover and ends with the Feast of Weeks.

ceremonies were passed on from generation to generation, but the meaning which was attached to them did not remain the same. There was a perennial source that kept the old meadows fresh.

They were taught to care for the most distant in the most immediate, knowing that the passing is a reflection of the lasting, that tables in their humble homes may become consecrated altars, that a single deed of one man may decide the fate of all men. Characteristic of their piety was the unheroic sacrifice—unassuming, inconspicuous devotion rather than extravagance, mortification, asceticism. The purpose was to ennoble the common, to endow worldly things with hieratic beauty.

A person scrupulously exact in observing the established rules and standards was considered to be a good Jew. But only one who went "beyond that which the law required" would approach the extraordinary.

Saintliness was not thought to consist in specific acts, such as in excessive prayer or performance of rituals, but was an attitude bound up with all actions, concomitant with all doings, accompanying and shaping all life's activities. Saintliness was not an excursion into spirituality. Its mark was loving-kindness. A saint was he who did not know how it is possible not to love, not to help, not to be sensitive to the anxiety of others.

Rabbi Israel Salanter, renowned thinker and founder of the "Moralist" movement, died in a foreign country, away from his numerous admirers and disciples. Only a very plain man, who took care of him while he was sick, was present when he passed away. Eager to learn what legacy of profound ideas the great scholar expounded in his last hours, the disciples questioned the attendant. All evening, the attendant told them, he tried to convince me that I should not be afraid to be left alone all night with the body of a dead man.[3]

For these people, Jewishness was more than a set of beliefs and rituals, more than what was compressed into tenets and rules. Jewishness was not in the fruit but in the sap that stirred through the tissues of the tree. Bred in the silence of the soil, it ascended to the leaves to become eloquent in the fruit. Jewishness was not only truth; it was vitality, joy; to some, the only joy. The intellectual majesty of the Shema Israel,[4] when translated into the language of their hearts, signified: "It is a joy to be a Jew."

[3] The body of a deceased person was never left alone until interment—, and superstitious people would experience fear when left alone with a body at night. This episode was told to Professor Saul Lieberman by Rabbi N. N. Finkel who heard it from the attendant.

[4] The confession of faith, recited twice daily: "Hear, O Israel, the Lord is our God, the Lord is One." (Deuteronomy 6:4.)

The East European Jews had a common will and a common destiny. They formed not merely a social group, but a community, full of color and contrasts, uniform in its variety. The Jews were like a land with many provinces — Litvaks,[5] Bessarabians, Ukrainians, and Galicians, Hasidim, Mithnaggdim,[6] Maskilim, Habadnikes,[7] Zionists, Agudists,[8] and Socialists — one language with many dialects. Social existence was complex, frequently dominated by centrifugal forces, but there was a common center and for the most part also a common periphery. There was enough social dynamism to create specific groupings. Hasidim, adherents of a particular *rebbe*,[9] even when residents of different cities and belonging to various economic strata, made up a group with a mode of life of its own, with peculiarities of thought, speech, and gestures, with customs and interests, which were at times so intensive that they even affected the social and economic status of the members of the group. Conversely, economic divisions often put their imprint on religious institutions. Artisans of a given trade established their own houses of worship, making themselves independent of the community synagogue.

[5] Lithuanian Jews.   [6] The opponents of Hasidim.
[7] A school within the Hasidic movement, founded by Rabbi Shneur Zalman of Ladi.
[8] Members of a political organization of Orthodox Jews.
[9] The title of a Hasidic leader.

The Two Great Traditions

IN THE PAST THOUSAND YEARS, TWO MA-JOR TRADITIONS FLOWERED IN JEWISH LIFE, CORRESPONDING TO THE TWO groups that have successively held the spiritual hegemony: first the Spanish Sephardic, and in the later period, the Ashkenazic.

The Sephardic group is composed of the descendants of Jews who settled in the Iberian Peninsula during the Mohammedan period. Spain is called in Hebrew *Sephard*, and these Jews therefore are known as Sephardim. Compelled to migrate and later expelled from Spain and Portugal in the fifteenth century, these Jews settled largely along the Mediterranean coast and in Holland, England, and their dependencies.

The Ashkenazic community includes the descendants of Jews who came from Babylon and Palestine to the Balkans and Central and Eastern Europe, and who since the later Middle Ages have spoken German or Yiddish. They are called Ashkenazic Jews, from the Hebrew word *Ashkenaz*, which means Germany.

Up to the nineteenth century, all Ashkenazic Jews who lived in the area bounded by the Rhine and the Dnieper and by the Baltic and the Black Sea, and in some neighboring regions as well, presented a culturally uniform group. At the center of this cultural period stood Rashi, the greatest commentator on the Bible and the Talmud, as well as Rabbi Jehudah the Pious and his circle. The spiritual development of the Ashkenazic period reached its climax in Eastern Europe, particularly with the spread of the Hasidic movement. Today the Ashkenazim form the preponderant majority of our people.

The Jews of the Iberian Peninsula were responsible for the earlier brilliant epoch in Jewish history, distinguished not only by monumental scientific achievements, but also by a universality of spirit. Their accomplishment was in some respects a synthesis of Jewish tradition and Moslem civilization.

The intellectual life of the Jews in Spain was deeply influenced by the surrounding world. Literary forms, scientific methods, philosophical categories, and even theological principles were often adopted from the Arabs. Stimulated and enriched in their writing and thinking by foreign patterns, Jewish authors were inclined to stress the basic agreements between the doctrines of their faith and the theories of great non-Jewish thinkers. Indeed, they often seemed to emphasize the elements Judaism had in common with classical philosophy to the neglect of pointing out its own specific features. They were under constant challenge and attack by members of other creeds, and felt compelled to debate and to defend the principles of their faith.

In the Ashkenazic period, the spiritual life of the Jews was lived in isolation. Accordingly, it grew out of its own ancient roots and developed in an indigenous environment, independent of the trends and conventions of the surrounding world. Intellectually more advanced than their average Germanic or Slavic neighbors, the Jews unfolded unique cultural patterns in thinking and writing, in their communal and individual ways of life. Tenaciously adhering to their own traditions, they concentrated upon the cultivation of what was most their own, what was most specific and personal. They borrowed from other cultures neither substance nor form. What they wrote was literature created by Jews, about Jews, and for Jews. They apologized to no one, neither to philosophers nor theologians, nor did they ask the commendation of either prince or penman. They felt no need to compare themselves with anyone else, and they wasted no energy in refuting hostile opinions.

There, in Eastern Europe, the Jewish people came into its own. It did not live like a guest in somebody else's house, who must constantly keep in mind the ways and customs of the host. There Jews lived without reservation and without disguise, outside their homes no less than within them. When they used the phrase "the world asks" in their commentaries on the Talmud, they did not refer to a problem raised by Aristotle or Averroes. Their fellow students of Torah were to them the "world."

The culture of Spanish Sephardic Jews was shaped by an elite; it was derived from above and was hardly touched by the archaic simplicity, imaginative naïveté, and unaffected naturalness of the humble mass.

In Spain, Jewish men of learning drew inspiration from classical philosophy and science. Frequently they took Arabic poetry and Greek ethics as prototypes. Jewish scholars were absorbed in theoretical research, designing their books frequently for limited groups, or even for single individuals. Their point of view was aristocratic. Their poems were often written in a Hebrew so complicated and involved that only the erudite could enjoy them. Under the influence of Arabic metric and rhetoric, the innate genius of Hebrew, with its chasteness, severity, and limpid strength, gave way to an arabesque manner. Writers reveled in fanciful, ornamental tropes that delight the fancy of the connoisseur rather than capture feeling. Employed to grace the façade of a sentence, words were grouped in fantastic combinations. And in books translated from the Arabic, the Hebrew was usually made to conform to the modes of the Arabic original.

On the lips of Ashkenazic Jews, however, Hebrew was freed from the golden chains of a complex rhetoric, and it came to be as easy and natural as the Hebrew of the authors of the Midrash in the early centuries of the common era. This Hebrew was not like a festive oriental carpet that is trod with measured step, but like a soft *tallith*,[1] a prayer shawl, at the same time sacred and common, in which you can wrap yourself

[1] A rectangular prayer shawl with fringes—*tsitsith*—attached to the four corners.

and be alone with your God. The Ashkenazim
did not write *piyutim*,[2] the elaborate and often
complicated liturgical poems favored by Sephardic authors; they wrote mostly *selihoth*,[3]
simple penitential prayers and elegies. They drew
their style from the homespun prose of Talmudic
sayings rather than from the lofty rhetoric of the
Prophets. The thunder of the Book of Job was
absent from their writings. Other rhythms and
other tones prevailed. The Hebrew of the Ashkenazic books on morality or piety was saturated
with the sadness, yearning, and contrition of the
Book of Psalms.

Further, the East European Jews created their
own language, Yiddish, which was born out of
a will to make intelligible, to explain and simplify
the tremendous complexities of the sacred literature. Thus there arose, as though spontaneously,
a mother tongue, a direct expression of feeling,
a mode of speech without ceremony or artifice, a
language that speaks itself without taking devi-
ous paths, a tongue that has a maternal intimacy
and warmth. In this language, you say "beauty"
and mean "spirituality"; you say "kindness" and
mean "holiness." Few languages can be spoken
so simply and so directly; there are but few lan-

[2] Synagogal poetry composed in the Middle Ages and recited during the services.
[3] Penitential prayers recited on fast days and after midnight or early in the morning during the penitential season.

guages which lend themselves with such difficulty to falseness. No wonder that Rabbi Nahman of Bratslav [4] would sometimes choose Yiddish to pour out his heart and present his yearnings to God. The Jews have spoken many languages since they went into exile; this was the only one they called "Jewish."

In the Sephardic period, every book or manuscript was a rare treasure. Few communities were fortunate enough to possess copies of all six sections of the Talmud. In the Ashkenazic period, Jews had all the texts; they made lavish use of the art of printing; books were published continually. The gates to the Torah were opened. Every community had the Talmud and the Code of Law, the Shulhan Arukh,[5] the legal system of Maimonides, and the classical work of Jewish mysticism, the Zohar.[6]

Numerous Spanish Jews had possessed high secular learning. Their original achievements in medicine, mathematics, and astronomy contributed greatly to the advancement of European civilization and through their translations of scientific and philosophical works from Arabic into

[4] A famous leader of Hasidim.
[5] "Set Table," the authoritative book on Jewish law, codified in the sixteenth century by Rabbi Joseph Caro.
[6] "Book of Splendor," the foremost work on Jewish mysticism, written in the form of a commentary on the Pentateuch.

Latin, they served as cultural mediators, making available to the European nations the treasures of literature and science then in Arab custody.

On the other hand, knowledge of Jewish lore does not seem to have been widespread among Spanish Jews. Young people were not accustomed to putting their minds exclusively to the study of the Torah. The educational programs drawn up for Jewish schools had but modest objectives. The celebrated poet and metaphysician, Rabbi Solomon Ibn Gabirol, complained that the people did not understand the sacred tongue. Rabbi Solomon Parhon, a grammarian who was a disciple of Rabbi Jehudah Halevi, wrote: "In our country (Spain) people are not well versed in the Hebrew language," while the Ashkenazic Jews "are accustomed to think and speak in Hebrew." Many Sephardic authors wrote largely in Arabic; even works dealing with questions of Jewish ritual, homilies on the Bible, commentaries on the Talmud, were written in Arabic. But to an Ashkenazic author, it would have seemed inconceivable to write his works in a foreign tongue.

Sephardic books are distinguished by their strict logical arrangement. Composed according to a clear plan, every one of their details has its assigned place, and the transitions from one subject to another are clear and simple. Ashkenazic writers forego clarity for the sake of depth. The contours of their thoughts are irregular, vague, and often perplexingly entangled; their content is restless, animated by inner wrestling and a kind of baroque emotion.

Sephardic books are like Raphaelesque paintings, Ashkenazic books like the works of Rembrandt—profound, allusive, and full of hidden meanings. The former favor the harmony of a system, the latter the tension of dialectic; the former are sustained by a balanced solemnity, the latter by impulsive inspiration. The strength of the Sephardic scholars lies in their mastery of expression, that of the Ashkenazim in the unexpressed overtones of their words. A spasm of feeling, a passionate movement of thought, an explosive enthusiasm, will break through the form.

Sephardic books are like neatly trimmed and cultivated parks, Ashkenazic writings like enchanted ancient forests; the former are like a story with a beginning and an end, the latter have a beginning but frequently turn into a story without an end.

The renowned painstaking grammarians of the Hebrew tongue came from among the Sephardim; the Ashkenazim were more interested in the dynamics of keen gematria—the art of finding implications believed to be contained in the numerical values of letters in Scripture—than in transparent, sober grammatical forms. In later times, critical, literal exegesis of Scripture almost disappeared.

Eminently concerned with preserving the Jewish spiritual heritage, the Sephardim were unsurpassed masters at systematizing, collating, and codifying the scattered multiplex wealth of Jewish lore accumulated in the course of previous ages. The Ashkenazim were less eager to collect than to disclose, to probe for deeper meanings; for them, the prime motive was not to know and remember, but to discover and understand; it was not the final decision that was important, but the steps of the syllogism whereby it was arrived at.

In the code of law, Mishneh Torah, composed by that foremost Sephardic master, Maimonides (1135–1204), the subject matter is arranged according to logical concepts; the stream of laws and precepts is converted into an abstract system. In the four Turim,[7] compiled by the Ashkenazi Rabbi Jacob, son of the Rosh (fourteenth century), which forms the basis of the Shulhan Arukh, the laws are arranged according to the daily routine of every Jew, beginning with his rising in the morning and ending with the night prayer, the Shema. Maimonides' system is logi-

[7] A code of Jewish Law written in the fourteenth century.

cal, but the Arba Turim is a mirror reflecting life as it is.

Classical books were not written in Eastern Europe. The Talmud, the Mishneh Torah, the Moreh Nebukhim,[8] the Zohar, and Ets Hayim[9] were produced in other countries. East European Jews did not cherish the ambition to create consummate, definitive expressions. And because their books were indigenous to their time and place and rooted in a self-contained world, they are less accessible to moderns than those of Sephardic authors. The Ashkenazim were not interested in writing literature; their works read like brief lecture notes. They were products, not of pure research, but of discussions with pupils. The Ashkenazim rarely composed books that stand like separate buildings with foundations of their own, books that do not lean upon older works; they wrote commentaries or notes on the classical works of olden times, books that modestly hug the monumental walls of older citadels.

The Sephardim aspired to personal perfection and attempted to express their ideals rationally. They strove for tranquillity of soul, for inner

[8] "The Guide of the Perplexed," Maimonides' work on the philosophy of Judaism.
[9] "The Tree of Life," a work on the mystical doctrine of Rabbi Isaac Luria, written by his disciple, Rabbi Hayim Vital (1543 1620).

peace and contentment. Their ethics was at times bourgeois, full of prudence and practical wisdom. To follow the golden rule, to take a middle course and avoid extremes, was one of their most popular maxims. The Kabbalah [10] remained a pursuit of the few; in contrast to the situation in Eastern Europe, the life of the people in the Sephardic community was hardly touched by the bold mystic doctrines of some of its rabbis.

Ashkenazic ethics, on the other hand, knew no perfection that was definable; its vision aimed at the infinite, never compromising, never satisfied, always striving—"Seek higher than that." The Ashkenazic moralist or Hasid was exalted; he yearned for the transcendental, the preternatural. He somehow felt that not only space, but also the soul was endless. Not for him the tranquil contemplation, the gradual ascent. What he sought was boundless fervor, praying and learning without limit or end. For though the seeker is engaged in a persistent struggle with the material and finite and cannot himself escape permanently, he can at least aspire to divest himself, in short moments of ecstasy, of all earthly concerns.

What distinguishes Sephardic from Ashkenazic culture is, however, primarily a difference of

[10] Jewish mysticism.

form rather than a divergence of content. It is a difference that cannot be characterized by the categories of rationalism versus mysticism or of the speculative versus the intuitive mentality. The difference goes beyond this and might be more accurately expressed as a distinction between a static form, in which the spontaneous is subjected to strictness and abstract order, and a dynamic form, which does not compel the content to conform to what is already established. The dynamic form is attained by subtler and more direct means. Room is left for the outburst, for the surprise, for the instantaneous. The inward counts infinitely more than the outward.

The dualism of Sephardic and Ashkenazic culture did not disappear with the tragic expulsion from Spain in 1492. The Sephardic strain, striving after measure, order, and harmony, and the Ashkenazic strain, with its preference for the spontaneous and dynamic, can both be traced down to the modern period. The Sephardim retained their independent ways in custom and thought and refused to amalgamate. In their seclusion, a severe loyalty to their heritage was combined with a feeling of pride in the splendor of their past. Their synagogue services were like silent mirrors of the ancient rite. The spontaneous was tamed, the unbecoming eliminated. But the continual trimming of the offshoots often tended to suppress any unexpected drive in the roots.

The Ashkenazic Jew, on the other hand, remained averse to forcing the fluent to unyielding forms. Kept spiritually alive by a sense of the immense rather than by a sense of balance, he would not yield to the admonitions of the few systematically minded scholars in his midst. The passion for the unlimited could not be conditioned by a regard for proportion and measure.

Much of what the Sephardim created was adopted by the Ashkenazim and transformed. Under the spell of the Hasidim, the rich and ponderous speculations of the Sephardic mystics were stripped of their tense and stern features without any loss of profundity or earnestness. The lofty and elaborate doctrines of the Kabbalah were melted into thoughts understandable by the heart.

In modern times, the Sephardic mentality was in a sense exemplified by Spinoza. Indeed, he owes many elements of his system to medieval Sephardic philosophy; and though he rejected its predominant aspirations, his thought pushed certain tendencies inherent in that tradition to extremes. His aristocratic intellectualism, for instance, led him to divide sharply between the piety and morality of the people and the speculative knowledge of the few. God is conceived of as a principle of mathematical necessity, a sort of

logical shell in which all things exist; logical thinking alone can bring men into a relation with God.
Personalism of any kind is excluded. It is remark-
able how limited was the influence of Spinoza's
philosophy even upon those Jewish thinkers who
departed from religious tradition.

Because the ideals of the Ashkenazic Jews were
shared by all, the relations between the various
parts of the community—between the scholarly
and the ignorant, the Yeshiva[11] student and the
trader—had an intimate organic character. The
earthiness of the villagers, the warmth of plain
people, and the spiritual simplicity of the *maggidim* or lay preachers penetrated into the *beth
ha-midrash*, the house of prayer that was also a
house of study and learning. Laborers, peasants,
porters, artisans, storekeepers, all were partners in
the Torah. The *maggidim*—the term presumably
originated in Eastern Europe—did not apply for
diplomas to anyone. They felt authorized by God
to be preachers of morals.

Here, in the Ashkenazic realm, the amalgama-
tion of Torah and Israel was accomplished. Ideals
became folkways, divine imperatives a human
concern; the people itself became a source of Judaism, a source of spirit. The most distant became
very intimate, very near. Spontaneously, without
external cause, the people improvised customs of

[11] A higher school of Talmudic learning.

celestial solemnity. The dictates of their own insight were heeded as commandments of highest authority. Jews began to know the meaning of "From within my flesh do I see the Lord." [12]

[12] Job 19:26.

For the People

AN INESTIMABLE FACTOR IN THE DE-VELOPMENT OF ASHKENAZIC JEWRY WAS THE DEMOCRATIZATION OF TALMUDIC learning to a degree unknown before.

In the first five centuries following the completion of the Talmud,[1] the Babylonian academies had hegemony over Jewish life. The Jews of all lands were accustomed to consult the Geonim, the celebrated heads of the academies of Sura and

---

[1] The body of Jewish law, legend and thought comprising the Mishnah, or text, and the Gemara, or commentary. It was completed in the fifth century.

Pumbeditha[2] on all points of earnest difficulty. Whenever they encountered an equivocal or obscure passage in the Talmud or a debatable issue of the law, or a problem of belief, they would send their question to Babylonia. The decisions, rulings, and interpretations of those eminent scholars were both authoritative and indispensable.

It was not until the twelfth century that the Occident began to emancipate itself. In that period, two epoch-making literary events changed the intellectual conditions of Jewish learning: Rashi composed his comprehensive commentary on the Talmud, and Maimonides published his Code of Jewish Law. They rendered the Jewish masses independent of the Geonim, whose office at the time began to decline. No longer was it necessary to refer questions to Babylonia. Maimonides created for the first time a compendium that covered the entire field of law, a masterpiece of construction, unsurpassed in the profundity of its decisions and implications, ingenious in the conciseness and simplicity of its style and brilliant in its omitting the argumentative and dialectical.

But it was particularly Rashi who brought intellectual emancipation to the people. Without a commentary, the Hebrew Scripture and partic-

[2] Town in Babylonia.

40

ularly the Talmud are accessible only to the enlightened few. The old commentaries offered interpretations of isolated passages and were mostly limited to single sections of the Talmud. Rashi's Commentary, explaining with exquisite simplicity almost every word of the immense text, unraveling the involved complexities of Talmudic dialectics, is a faithful companion who attends the student to whatever part of the text he may turn. Humbly, unobtrusively, he communes with the student, conveying by a minimum of words a maximum of meaning. With the help of a short phrase or even one word, he frequently illumines what seems to be thick darkness. Instead of offering abstract dissertations on principles, methods, and legal decisions, he explains only what immediately concerns the student, the meaning of a term, the implication of a statement, the gist of an intricate argument.

Rashi *democratized* Jewish education, he brought the Bible, the Talmud, and the Midrash[3] to the people. He made the Talmud a popular book, everyman's book. Learning ceased to be the monopoly of the few. It spread increasingly with the passing of time. In many communities, the untutored became the rare exception.

[3] Works of exposition on the Bible, written during the first millennium.

In almost every Jewish home in Eastern Europe, even in the humblest and the poorest, stood a bookcase full of volumes; proud and stately folio tomes together with shy, small-sized books. Books were neither an asylum for the frustrated nor a means for occasional edification. They were furnaces of living strength, timeproof receptacles for the eternally valid coins of spirit. Almost every Jew gave of his time to learning, either in private study or by joining one of the societies established for the purpose of studying the Talmud or some other branch of rabbinic literature. To some people, it was impossible to pray without having been refreshed first by spending some time in the sublime atmosphere of Torah.[4] Others, after the morning prayer, would spend an hour with their books before starting to work. At nightfall, almost every one would leave the tumult and bustle of everyday life to study in the *beth ha-midrash*. Yet the Jews did not feel themselves to be "the People of the Book." They did not feel that they possessed the "Book," just as one does not feel that one possesses life. The Book, the Torah, was their essence, just as they, the Jews, were the essence of the Torah.

A typical Jewish township in Eastern Europe was "a place where Torah has been studied from time immemorial; where practically all the inhab-

[4] Divine instruction or guidance; Scripture; Jewish lore.

itants are scholars, where the Synagogue or the House of Study is full of people of all classes busily engaged in studies, townfolk as well as young men from afar . . . where at dusk, between twilight and evening prayers, artisans and other simple folk gather around the tables to listen to a discourse on the great books of Torah, to interpretations of Scripture, to readings from theological, homiletical, or ethical writings like Hovoth Ha-Levavoth[5] and the like . . . where on the Sabbath and the holidays, near the Holy Ark, at the reading stand, fiery sermons are spoken that kindle the hearts of the Jewish people with love for the Divine Presence, sermons which are seasoned with words of comfort from the prophets, with wise parables and keen aphorisms of the sages, in a voice and a tone that heartens one's soul, that melts all limbs, that penetrates the whole being."[6]

Poor Jews, whose children knew only the taste of "potatoes on Sunday, potatoes on Monday, potatoes on Tuesday," sat there like intellectual magnates. They possessed whole treasures of thought, a wealth of information, of ideas and sayings of many ages. When a problem came up, there was immediately a host of people, pouring

[5] "The Duties of the Heart," a work on Jewish piety, written by Rabbi Bahya ibn Pakuda in the eleventh century.
[6] From "Shloime Reb Hayim's" by Mendele Moher Sefarim, one of the great Hebrew and Yiddish writers.

out opinions, arguments, quotations. One raised a question on a controversial passage in Maimonides' work, and many vied with one another in attempts to explain it, outdoing one another in the subtlety of dialectic distinctions or in citing out-of-the-way sources. The stomachs were empty, the homes barren, but the minds were crammed with the riches of Torah.

The Luxuries of Learning

HERE WERE MANY WHO LIVED IN AP-PALLING POVERTY, MANY WHO WERE PINCHED BY NEVER-ENDING WORRIES, and there were plenty of taverns with strong spirits. But drunkards were rarely seen among Jews. When night came and a man wanted to pass away time, he did not hasten to a tavern to take a drink, but went to pore over a book or joined a group which—either with or without a teacher—indulged in the enjoyment of studying revered books. Physically worn out by their day's toil, they sat over open volumes, playing the austere music of the Talmud's groping for truth or the sweet melodies of exemplified piety of ancient sages.

"Once I noticed," writes a Christian scholar, who visited the city of Warsaw during the First World War, "a great many coaches on a parking-place but with no drivers in sight. In my own country I would have known where to look for them. A young Jewish boy showed me the way: in a courtyard, on the second floor, was the *shtibl* of the Jewish drivers. It consisted of two rooms: one filled with Talmud-volumes, the other a room for prayer. All the drivers were engaged in fervent study and religious discussion. . . . It was then that I found out and became convinced that all professions, the bakers, the butchers, the shoemakers, etc., have their own *shtibl* in the Jewish district; and every free moment which can be taken off from their work is given to the study of the Torah. And when they get together in intimate groups, one urges the other: '*Sog mir a shtickl Torah*—Tell me a little Torah.'"

An old book saved from the countless libraries recently burned in Europe, now at the Yivo[1] Library in New York, bears the stamp, "The

[1] Yiddish Scientific Institute.

Society of Wood-Choppers for the Study of Mishnah [2] in Berditshev."

They were a people whose most popular lullaby chants: "The Torah is the highest good." Mothers at the cradles crooned: "My little child, close your eyes; if God will, you'll be a rabbi." The state did not have to compel the Jews to send their children to school. Joshua had commanded the children of Israel to study the Torah "day and night."

At the birth of a baby, the school children would come and chant the Shema Israel in unison around the cradle. When taken for the first time to the *heder*, [3] the child was wrapped in a prayer shawl like a scroll. Schoolboys were referred to as "the holy flock," and a mother's tenderest pet name for a boy was "my little *zaddik*," my little saint. Parents were ready to sell the pillow from under their heads to pay tuition for their children; a poorly educated father wanted at least his children to be scholars. Women toiled day and night to enable their husbands to devote themselves to study. When economic exigencies made it impossible for people to give most of their time to the Torah, they tried at least to support the students. They shared their scanty food to give board

[2] The earliest part of the Talmud, containing the fundamentals of Jewish law.
[3] Elementary Hebrew school.

to a wandering student. And when the melancholy, sweet chanting of Talmudic study coming from the *beth ha-midrash* penetrated the neighboring streets, exhausted Jews on their pallets felt sweet delight at the thought that by their acts of support they had a share in that learning. In small towns, the sexton would go at dawn from house to house, knocking at the shutters and chanting:

> Get up, Jews,
> Sweet, holy Jews,
> Get up and worship the Creator!
> God is in exile,
> The Shekinah [4] is in exile,
> The people is in exile.
> Get up to serve the Creator!

The ambition of every Jew was to have a scholar as a son-in-law, and a man versed in the Torah could easily marry a well-to-do girl and obtain *kest* [5] for a few years or even permanently, and thus have the good fortune of being able to study in peace. Nowadays we speak disparagingly of this custom. But few institutions have

---

[4] "Indwelling." Divine hypostasis indwelling in the world and sharing the exile of Israel; Divine Presence among men; a synonym for God.

[5] The part of the dowry which consisted of a promise to provide food and board for a specified number of years after the marriage.

done more to promote the spiritual development of large masses of people.

Their learning was essentially nonutilitarian, almost free of direct pragmatic designs, an aesthetic experience. They delved into those parts of the lore that had no relevance to daily life no less eagerly than into those that had a direct bearing on it. Detached in their learning from interests in mundane affairs, they grappled with problems which were remote from the banalities of the normal course of living. He who studied for the purpose of receiving a rabbinical diploma was the object of ridicule. In the eyes of these people, knowledge was not a means for achieving power, but a way of clinging to the source of all reality. In the eyes of Hasidim, study for the sake of acquiring scholarship was considered a desecration.

The aim was to partake of spiritual beauty, or to attain by osmosis a degree of self-purification. Carried away by the mellow, melting chant of Talmud reading, one's mind would soar high in pure realm of thought, away from this world of facts and worries, away from the boundaries of here and now, to a region where the Shekinah listens to what the children of men create in the study of His Word. There was holiness in their acumen, the cry "my soul thirsteth for God, the living God"[6] in their wrestling with the Lore.

[6] Psalm 42:2.

They were able to feel heaven in a passage of Talmud.

Rabbi Zusya[7] of Hanipol once started to study a volume of the Talmud. A day later, his disciples noticed that he was still dwelling on the first page. They assumed that he must have encountered a difficult passage and was trying to solve it. But when a number of days passed and he was still immersed in the first page, they were astonished, but did not dare to query the master. Finally one of them gathered courage and asked him why he did not proceed to the next page. And Rabbi Zusya answered: "I feel so good here, why should I go elsewhere?"

[7] A Hasidic leader.

Pilpul

ENAMORED OF LEARNING, THEY PUT THEIR ENTIRE BEING INTO THE STUDY OF THE TALMUD. THEIR INTELLECTUAL EFFORT was stirred by a blazing passion. It is an untold, perhaps incommunicable, story of how mind and heart could merge into one. Immersed in complicated legal discussions, they could at the same time feel the anguish of Shekinah that abides in exile. Endeavoring to solve an antinomy or contradiction raised by a seventeenth-century supercommentary on the Talmud, they were able in the same breath to throb with sympathy for Israel and all people afflicted with distress. Study was a technique of sublimating feeling into thought, of transposing dreams into syllogisms, of expressing grief in formulating keen theoretical difficulties and joy in finding a solution to a difficult passage in Maimonides. Tension of the soul found an outlet in contriving sagacious, almost insoluble riddles. They invented new logical devices in explaining the word of God, thrilled with yearning after the Holy. To figure out an answer to gnawing doubts was to them supreme pleasure. Indeed, a world of subdued gaiety and frolic quivered in the playful subtleties of their *pilpul*.

Pilpul, the characteristic method of study developed in the East European period, had its origin at the ancient academies in Babylonia in the first centuries of the common era. Its goal was not to acquire information about the Law, but rather to examine its implications and presuppositions; not just to absorb and to remember but to discuss and to expand. All later doctrines were considered to be tributaries of the ancient never-failing stream of tradition. One could debate with the great sages of bygone days. There was no barrier between the past and the present. If disagreement was discovered between a view held by Rabbi Akiba Eiger of Posen, who lived in the nineteenth century, and Rabbi Isaac Alfassi of Morocco, who lived in the eleventh century, a

Warsaw scholar of the twentieth century would intervene to prove the consistency in the learning carried on throughout the ages.

The power of the *pilpul* penetrated even into the Kabbalah. Dialectic joined with mysticism. The later Ashkenazic kabbalists constructed symbolic labyrinths out of mystic signs so involved that only Kabbalists endowed with both mystic passion and intellectual keenness could safely venture into them.

The plain meaning of words, the straight line of a general rule seemed too shallow, too thin, too narrow to hold the expanding power of their minds. In the light of the *pilpul*, the nature and force of words and concepts underwent a radical change. The simplest principle was disclosed to rest upon a complex of concepts and involved in a mass of relations to other principles. New conclusions of old rules heretofore unnoticed were thus deduced, offering guidance in cases which had not been provided for in old works. At the same time, inconsistencies and divergencies were revealed by applying an even more penetrating and minute analysis of the subject matter.

At times, the *pilpul* degenerated into hairsplitting dialectics and grappled with intellectual phantoms. Deviating from the conventional forms of logical soundness, it was bitterly attacked by some of the great rabbis. Yet, not only did the *pilpul* infuse new vitality into the study of the Talmud, it stimulated ingenuity and independence of mind, encouraging the students to create new out of old ideas. Over and above that, the storm of the soul that was held in check by rigorous discipline, the inner restlessness, found a vent in flights of the intellect. Thinking became full of vigor, charged with passion. The mind melted the metal of Talmudic ideas and forged it into fantastic molds, zigzags, in which thought at first became startled, lost its way, but at the end succeeded in disentangling itself. They did not know how to take anything for granted. Everything had to have a reason, and they were more interested in reasons than in things.

Ideas were like precious stones. The thought that animated them reflected a wealth of nuances and distinctions, as the ray of light passing through a prism produces the colors of the rainbow. Upon rotation, many-faceted ideas shed a glittering brilliance that varied in accordance with the direction in which they were placed against the light of reason. The alluring gracefulness, the variety of the polished ideas enlightened the intellect, dazzled the eye. Concepts acquired a dynamic quality, a color and meaning that, at first thought, seemed to have no connection with one another. The joy of discovery, the process of inventing original devices, of attaining new inventions and new insights, quickened and elated the heart. This was not realistic thinking; but great art likewise is not a reproduction of nature, nor is mathematics an imitation of something that actually exists.

It is easy to belittle such an attitude of mind and to call it unpractical, unworldly. But what is nobler than the unpractical spirit? The soul is sustained by the regard for that which transcends all immediate purposes. The sense of the transcendent is the heart of culture, the very essence of humanity. A civilization that is devoted exclusively to the utilitarian is at bottom not different from barbarism. The world is sustained by unworldliness.

SEVEN

A World of Palimpsests

TO THEM, HISTORY WAS ONLY AN INTIMA-
TION. THINGS WERE LIKE PALIMPSESTS,
HEAVEN THE TANGENT AT THE CIRCLE OF
all experience. They were sure that everything
hinted at something transcendent, that what was
apparent to the mind is but a thin surface of the
undisclosed, and they often preferred to gain a
foothold on the brink of the deep even at the price
of leaving the solid ground of the superficial.

The words of the Torah, they believed, would
not be grasped by means of literal interpretation.
Nothing could be taken literally, neither Scripture

nor nature. No man, even if he lived a thousand years, would be able to fathom the mysteries of the world. Rabbi Nathan Spira of Cracow, the author of "The Revealer of the Deeply Hidden," written in the seventeenth century, interprets in two hundred and fifty-two different ways the portion of the Pentateuch in which Moses pleads with God for permission to enter the Promised Land. A Biblical word, a custom or a saying, was thought to be crammed with a multiplicity of meaning. The plain was too shallow to be true. Only the mystery was plausible, while the one-dimensional, the superficial was inconceivable. Everywhere they found cryptic meaning.

Even in the part of the Code dealing with civil and criminal law, they discovered profound mysteries. Allusions were found in names of towns and countries. The name of Poland was allegedly derived from the two Hebrew words *po-lin*, "here abide," which were inscribed on a note descended from heaven and found by the refugees from Germany on their eastward journey at the time of the Black Death and the attendant massacres of Jews. On the leaves of the trees, the story goes, were inscribed sacred names, and in the branches were hidden errant souls seeking deliverance through the intermediation of a pious Jew, who in passing would stop to say his twilight prayer under the tree.

Considering the itinerary of one's life, who could comprehend where the goals lie? One might go on a journey for the purpose of transacting business, while the true end was to worship in an inn, where the thought of God had never pierced the air, or to render help to a weary man encountered on the road. One might fulfill his destiny by the way.

Once, it is told, Rabbi Israel Baal Shem, the founder of the Hasidic movement, looked despondent and sick at heart. When his disciples asked him for the cause, he told them: There was a man who was very wicked. After he died, there was no way of saving him. But God had mercy upon his soul, and it was decreed that it should be incarnated in a frog and lie near a spring in a distant land, and should his son ever come to that place and drink of the water of the spring after saying the blessing over the water, the soul would be redeemed. But the son was very poor and had neither the means nor the opportunity to travel to distant places, so God caused that he should become the butler of a rich man who once became ill, and the doctors declared that he would be cured, if he went to a certain spa. The rich man went there and took his butler with him. Once while taking a walk together, the butler became unbearably thirsty—he almost died of thirst. (His thirst was so great because he was near the spring where the soul of his father was lying.) When he began to search for water he found a spring. In his great thirst, he forgot to say the prayer, the blessing over the water, and the soul remained unredeemed. . . . The Holy One, blessed be He, concluded the Baal Shem, did so much to make the redemption of the soul possible, yet all was in vain. Who knows what will be the end of its way?

Just as their thinking was distinguished by the reaching out for the most subtle, so was their mode of expression marked by a tendency toward terseness, particularly of those engaged in mystic lore. Their sayings were pointed, aiming at an idea in one bound, instead of approaching it gradually and slowly. The East European Jews had a predilection for elliptic sentences, for the incisive, epigrammatic form, for the flash of the mind, for the thunderclap of an idea. They spoke briefly, sharply, quickly and directly; they understood each other with a hint; they heard two words where only one was said. Mentioning the more obvious of two premises was considered trite.

Audacious doctrines were disguised as allegories or even witty maxims, and a seeming commonplace often contained a sublime thought. Holy men seemed to be discussing the building of a roof; they spoke of bricks and shingles, while they were actually debating the mysteries of the Torah. Whole theories of life were implied in simple stories told at tea after the *havdalah* ceremony, which marked the end of the Sabbath. Jokes without a deeper meaning were considered tasteless; the type of humor that was truly appreciated was a tale from which a meaning suddenly emerged like a charming glade opening in a forest.

The characteristic feature of their wit was intellectualism. Play upon words, such as Heine's famous witticism, "I was sitting next to Rothschild and he treated me just as an equal, quite famillionaire," may well serve as an example of what was *alien* to the spirit of their humor. Puns are almost absent in Yiddish, and in Hebrew they are used not in wit making, but in the serious quest of symbolic associations. Nor was bodily weakness or deformity an object of humor. They laughed not so much at the incongruity of some accident, at the awkwardness of a situation, as at preconceived notions and illogical inventions. The favorite tendency of their wit was to ridicule logical rather than verbal fallacies. Their jokes could serve as perfect illustrations of fallacies as defined and classified in formal logic.

The Deed Sings

WE MUST UNDERSTAND THE SENSE OF VALUES THAT CHARACTERIZED THE EAST EUROPEAN JEWS IN ORDER TO APPRAISE the fact that their best intellects were devoted to the study, interpretation, and development of the Torah. In their eyes, the world was not a derelict which the creator had abandoned to chance. Life to them was not an opportunity for indulgence, but a mission entrusted to every individual, an enterprise at least as responsible, for example, as the management of a factory. Every man constantly produces thoughts, words, deeds, committing them either to the powers of holiness or the powers of impurity. He is constantly engaged either in building or in destroying. But his task is to restore, by fulfilling the Torah, what has been impaired in the cosmos, to labor in the service of the cosmos for the sake of God.

The East European scholar was rarely dominated by a desire for austere rigorism or a liking for irrational discipline as a purpose in itself. In the main, he was inspired by a sense of the importance of his mission and by the conviction that the world could not exist without the Torah. This sense lent his life the quality of an artistic act, the medium of which is not stone or bronze, but the mystic substance of the universe.

Scientists dedicate their lives to the study of the habits of insects or the properties of plants. To them every trifle is significant; they inquire diligently into the most intricate qualities of things. But the pious Ashkenazic scholars investigated just as passionately the laws that ought to govern human conduct. The relentless honesty and painstaking devotion invested in their studies have, indeed, their analogy in the work of scientists. Wishing to banish the chaos of human existence and to civilize the life of man according to the Torah, they trembled over every move, every breath; no detail was treated lightly—everything was serious. Just as the self-sacrificing devotion of the scientist seems torture to the debauchee, so the poetry of rigorism jars on the ears of the cynic. But, perhaps, the question of what benediction to pronounce upon a certain type of food, the problem of matching the material with the spiritual, is more important than is generally imagined.

Man has not advanced very far from the coast of chaos. A frantic call to disorder shrieks in the world. Where is the power that can offset the effect of that alluring call? The world cannot remain a vacuum. We are all either ministers of the sacred or slaves of evil. The only safeguard against constant danger is constant vigilance, constant guidance.

Unfree men are horrified by the suggestion of accepting a spiritual regimen. Associating inner control with external tyranny, they would rather suffer than be subject to spiritual authority. Only free men, ready to abandon caprice, do not equate self-restraint with self-surrender.

It would be a mistake to characterize the piety of the East European Jew as an attitude of self-restraint. The clear perception of spiritual significance in observing the law made self-restraint unnecessary. The pleasurableness of "good deeds" made many of them wonder whether the reward for their fulfillment, promised by the rabbis in the life to come, would not be undeserved.

A woman was pouring out her heart to the rabbi of Tel Aviv. Her sons had abandoned religious observance. They were Halutzim, pioneers who gave up studies and careers to drain the swamps of the Holy Land. "I know," she said, "that my sons are holy people and am sure they will inherit the world to come. But I feel distressed at the fact that they do not enjoy the pleasures of this world as well, the pleasures of observing the Jewish law."

To the uninspired, the Shulhan Arukh is like the score of an oratorio to those who cannot read musical notations; to the pious Jew, it is full of choruses and arias. Jewish law to him is sacred music. The Divine sings in noble deeds. Man's effort is but the counterpoint to the music of His will.

There is a price to be paid by the Jew. He has to be exalted in order to be normal. In order to be a man, he has to be more than a man. To be a people, the Jews have to be more than a people.

The Devout Men of Ashkenaz

AS RASHI DEMOCRATIZED JEWISH EDUCA-
TION, SO IN THE TWELFTH AND THIR-
TEENTH CENTURIES, RABBI JEHUDAH
he-Hasid and his circle of Hasidim, "the pious,"
democratized the ideals of mystic piety. No high
intellectual powers were necessary for the attain-
ment of these ideals: the main requirements being
faith, a pure heart, inwardness. Piety was thought
to be more important than wisdom; candor
ranked higher than speculation; the God-fearing
man above the scholar. By their apotheosis of simplicity, of warm faith, of humaneness, and moral

65

devotion, they paved a highway to God for plain mortals.

The importance of prayer was unceasingly stressed by these medieval Hasidim. The prayer book, the *siddur*, a work that has more folk quality than any other in our literature, was passionately dear to them; every word in it a precious jewel. They counted the words of the *siddur*, because in them, it was believed, was contained a world of mysteries. They tried to uncover the old secrets that the prophets (as we are told by Rabbi Eleazar Rokeah of Worms, a thirteenth-century mystic) transmitted to their disciples, and which were later handed down from mouth to mouth, revealed to the chosen few.

However, the concentration upon the secrets was not the major aim. The awkward but heartfelt prayer of the simple, untutored man stands higher in value than the pedantic and ceremonious prayers of the man of learning.

A Hasid was taught to be forbearing with all the world, to be patient, mild, and gentle in judging others, to love man as well as animals, to be shy, bashful, and to avoid honors and social distinction, to serve God for the sake of God rather than for reward. Constant self-scrutiny and repentance assumed a place of prominence in Hasidic piety unknown before, with ascetic exercises as indispensable means of repentance.

Even if one did not feel burdened with a load of his own sins, he should repent the sins of others.

The "Devout Men of Ashkenaz" attached great importance to the customs—*minhaggim*—adopted by pious people, to usages that had not been derived from scholastic interpretations of texts, but had been improvised independently, instinctively. They began to commit to writing the customs of various individuals and communities. Books were composed for the purpose of teaching the people tact, good manners, and courtesy toward one's fellow men. In this spirit, books specially designed for the ordinary folk were written, poetic and gentle in style and abounding in folk tales and parables. They did not discuss high ideals in the abstract, but preached morality in a popular fashion. There arose a whole literature in *Teitsh*—Yiddish—for women. For centuries, Jewish women read the *Lev Tov*, "Good Heart" and the *Ze-enah Ure-enah*, "Go Forth and Behold," and poured out their hearts in *tehinoth*, tender devotional prayers, written by women for women.

The times were hard, the Jews were persecuted and hunted on all sides. Massacres were almost a daily occurrence; they were slaughtered like sheep. But the Jews patiently bore their lot and with a superhuman ardor sacrificed themselves for their faith. The Sefer Hasidim, "Book of the Devout," containing the maxims and sayings of the Ashkenazic Hasidim, finds it necessary to comfort those who "die on their beds" and are denied the privilege of dying for the Sanctification of the Name. Life at its best is lived on a spiritual battlefield. Man must constantly struggle with the evil inclination—"for man is like unto a rope, one end of which is pulled by God and the other end by Satan." Hence the Jew must learn the tactics of this war. He has to eschew all but the essentials of life, avoid and withstand temptations. And if one stumbled, God forbid, his lapses could be atoned for by mortification and an adequate number of fast days, which help to purge the soul of its stain.

For that reason, renowned scholars sometimes closed their Talmud volumes and set out wandering to live in self-imposed "exile," far from home, among strangers, to bear humiliation and taste the cup of privation and misery.

Kaballah

IN THE SEVENTEENTH CENTURY, THE MYSTIC TEACHINGS OF THE ZOHAR AND OF RABBI ISAAC LURIA OF SAFED BEGAN TO penetrate into Poland. The rabbis gave permission to print the esoteric books, and the people were seized with a desire to study the Kabbalah, which had heretofore been known only to a few individuals and was now available to all.

The spread of mysticism exerted a deep influence on the life of the East European Jews. The Kabbalah gave them a new sense, the sense of the all-pervading mystery.

To the analytical mind, the universe is broken apart. It is split into the known and unknown, into the seen and unseen. But, in the mystic contemplation, all things are seen as one. The mystic mind tends to hold the world together: to behold the seen in conjunction with the unseen, to keep the fellowship with the unknown through the revolving door of the known. The Kabbalists knew that what their senses perceive is but the jutting edge of what is deeply hidden. Extending over into the invisible, the things of this world stand in a secret contact with that which no eye has ever perceived. Everything certifies to the sublime, the unapparent working jointly with the apparent. There is always a reverberation in the beyond to every action here. All things below are symbols of that which is above. They are sustained by the forces that flow from hidden worlds. The worldly is subservient to the otherworldly. You grasp the essence of the here by conceiving the beyond—for this world is the reality of the spirit in a state of trance. The manifestation of the mystery is partly suspended, with ourselves living in lethargy. Normal consciousness is a state of stupor, in which sensibility to the wholly real and responsiveness to the stimuli of the spirit are reduced. The mystics, knowing that man is involved in a hidden history of the cosmos, endeavor to awake from the drowsiness and apathy and to regain the state of wakefulness for their enchanted souls.

To the Kabbalists, the difference between the known and the unknown, between the "revealed" and the "hidden," between the limited and the unlimited, was blurred. The familiar and habitual was conceived as floating in the mighty stream of mysteries and infinity, and men became aware of the sea in which the world is but a drop.

Attachment to hidden worlds held the Kabbalists in the spell of things more basic than the things that dominate the interest of the common mind. Inspired by the idea that not only is God necessary to man, but that man is also necessary to God, that man's actions are vital to all worlds and affect the course of transcendent events, the Kabbalistic preachers and popular writers sought to imbue all people with the consciousness of the supreme importance of all actions. It became a matter of popular conviction that what takes place "above" in the upper sphere, depends upon man "below." By every holy action, by every pure thought, man intervenes in the "supernal worlds." A pious deed is a mystery. By virtue of the devotion invested in it man constantly builds spiritual worlds, the essence of which the mind, as long as he is still of this world, cannot conceive. But his deeds are relevant not only for the upper spheres, but for this world as well. An architect of hidden worlds, every pious Jew is, partly, the messiah.

According to the Kabbalah, redemption is not an event that will take place all at once at "the end of days" nor something that concerns the Jewish people alone. It is a continual process, taking place at every moment. Man's good deeds are single acts in the long drama of redemption, and not only the people of Israel, but the whole universe must be redeemed. Even the Shekinah itself, the Divine Indwelling, is in exile. God is involved, so to speak, in the tragic state of this world; the Shekinah "lies in dust." The feeling of the presence of the Shekinah in human suffering became indelibly engraved in the consciousness of the East European Jews. To bring about the restitution of the universe was the goal of all efforts.

The meaning of man's life lies in his perfecting the universe. He has to distinguish, gather, and redeem the sparks of holiness scattered throughout the darkness of the world. This service is the motive of all precepts and good deeds. Man holds the keys that can unlock the chains fettering the Redeemer. But the Jew, upon whom the deliverance of the world is incumbent, is in a position not merely to build but also to destroy. Endowed with gigantic strength, he can through proper consecration ascend to the highest spheres; his spirit can create heavens. At the same time, however, he must not forget that his feet are upon the ground, close to the powers of darkness. It can easily come to pass that an evil urge may suddenly take hold of him and that instead of ascending to heaven he may be cast down into the abyss.

Every sin brings into being a demonic force, endowed with life and vicious power, seeking to enhance the reality of evil, to harm and mislead all men. It is horrifying to live in this world of ours, where the atmosphere is crowded with the immense population of malicious beings begotten of evil deeds. And all this peril and hostility is man's own creation.

Never before in Jewish history was the sense of the power of evil so haunting and keen as in the seventeenth and eighteenth centuries in Eastern Europe. As a consequence of that consciousness and strongly convinced of man's ultimate superiority to the power of evil, the Jews mobilized their might, attempting to subdue the foe within the heart, the appeal of brute matter. They fasted every Monday and Thursday and underwent fierce mortifications to purify themselves. The evil urge, they believed, pursues every man, ready to make him stumble at any false step. This state of mind led both to rapture and to sadness: the Jews felt the infinite beauty of heaven, the holy mysteries of piety, and also the danger and gloom of this world. Man is so unworthy and disgraceful and the heavens are so lofty and remote—what must man do in order not to fall into the Nethermost Pit?

ELEVEN

Hasidim

HEN CAME RABBI ISRAEL BAAL SHEM, IN THE EIGHTEENTH CENTURY, AND BROUGHT HEAVEN DOWN TO EARTH. HE and his disciples, the Hasidim, banished melancholy from the soul and uncovered the ineffable delight of being a Jew. God is not only the creator of earth and heaven. He is also the One "who created delight and joy." "And when we talk about the need of joy," says one of the great Hasidic thinkers, "we do not mean the joy that is felt in fulfilling the commandments, for the ability of spontaneously feeling such a joy is a privilege of illustrious souls and one cannot demand that every Jew be illustrious. What we mean is, to be free of sadness. A Jew who does not rejoice in the fact of his being a Jew is ungrateful toward heaven; it is a sign that he has failed to grasp the meaning of having been born a Jew." Even lowly merriment has its ultimate origin in holiness. The fire of evil can be better fought with flames of ecstasy than through fasting and mortification.

Jewishness was as though reborn. Bible verses, observances, customs, suddenly took on a flavor like that of new grain. A new prohibition was added: "Thou shalt not be old!" The Baal Shem rejuvenated us by a thousand years. The Jews fell in love with the Lord and felt "such yearning for God that it was unbearable."

They began to feel the infinite sweetness that comes with the fulfilling of the precept of hospitality or of wearing the *tallith* and *tefillin*.[1] What meaning is there to the life of a Jew, if it is not to acquire the ability to feel the taste of heaven? He who does not taste paradise in the performance of a precept in this world will not feel the taste of paradise in the world to come. And

[1] Leather cubicles containing scriptural texts inscribed on parchment. In accordance with the commandment in Deuteronomy 11:18, *tefillin* are attached to the left arm and to the head during the weekday morning service. They are a sign of the covenant between God and Israel.

so the Jews began to feel life everlasting in a sacred melody and to absorb the Sabbath as a vivid anticipation of the life to come.

There was great excitement in Strelisk. Hasidim danced in the streets. Rabbi Mendel, the rebbe of Kossov, had arrived to spend a day with his brother-in-law, Rabbi Uri the Seraph,[2] the rebbe of Strelisk. It was well known that to these two *zaddikim*—saintly men—the gates of heaven were open. The rebbe of Kossov held the key to the celestial Treasury of Sustenance, and whoever received his blessing no longer had to worry about the necessities of life. The Seraph, on the other hand, held the key to the Treasury of Saintliness. As a result, the Hasidim or adherents of the rebbe of Kossov were all well-to-do, some of them even wealthy, while the Hasidim of the Seraph were very saintly, but extremely poor. But a happy folk they were—the Hasidim of the Seraph. They were thrilled to live in his presence and reveled in the joys and ecstasies of prayer and the service of God. Three times a day would wage the great battle of prayer into which they would throw themselves with undaunted courage, as if they aimed to storm hidden fortresses of heaven. And when the battle was over, they

[2] The title by which he is known to this day, given to him because of his fiery soul and his perpetual fervor.

were exhausted and amazed at the wonder of having survived.

The rebbe of Kossov, the distinguished guest, was shocked at the sight of the extreme poverty in which the Hasidim of the Seraph lived. He had heard of their indigence, but what he saw—the emaciated bodies, the tattered clothes—surpassed his imagination. Angrily he turned to his brother-in-law: "Why do you permit this?" "Believe me, I am not to blame. They do not really feel any want," answered the latter in apology.

This answer did not satisfy the rebbe of Kossov. Late at night, after the great celebration for the honored guest was over and the songs and dances came to an end, he let it be known that all Hasidim of the Seraph should come to see him.

"What, for example, would be your most cherished desire?" he asked them. The Hasidim were embarrassed. Their most cherished desire, of course, was to attain perfect saintliness, to be able to say at least one prayer in the same spirit as their rebbe. But who would even dare to dream of such unattainable aims? So the rebbe of Kossov became specific: "What about sustenance?" This came as a surprise. Yes, they agreed, it would be a good thing not to be in want. They thought of their wives, of dowries for their grown-up daughters. "Listen," the rebbe of Kossov announced, "tomorrow during the morning service whatever you will pray for will be fulfilled."

It was a night full of excitement. They spent restless hours repeating to themselves and fixing in their minds the desire for sustenance, *lest they forget to pray for it*. Here was a chance that might never occur again.

Early next morning when the Seraph appeared in the synagogue, roaring like a lion, "*Adon Alom*—Eternal Lord," the Hasidim joined in the vehement encounter. Their songs all but tore the world apart, and they almost lost their souls on the way to heaven, in complete oblivion of the theme they had rehearsed the previous night. . . .

After the service, gradually recovering from their exhaustion, they realized to their dismay: "Ah, ah! Forgotten, completely forgotten!"[3]

The Hasidim attained so much inner strength that they ceased to dread the flesh. Do not inflict pain upon it, do not torment it—one should pity the flesh. "Hide not thyself from thine own flesh."[4] One can serve God even with the body, even with the evil inclination; one must only be able to distinguish between dross and gold. This

[3] This story, which I heard from Rabbi A. J. Heschel of Kopcsynce, is now narrated by B. Hager, *Ojfn Weg*, Bucuresti, 1946.   [4] Isaiah 58:7.

world acquires flavor only when a little of the other world is mingled with it. Without nobility, the flesh is full of darkness. The Hasidim have always maintained that the joys of this world were not the highest one could achieve, and they fanned in themselves the passion for spirituality, the yearning for the joys of the world to come.

In life on earth man is able to experience both this world and the world to come, and one should never mistake worldly for supreme joys, the earth for heaven.

There is a story of a *melammed* [5] making a pilgrimage on foot to see his rebbe who lived in a distant town. It was wintertime. The way was weary and the weather was grim. Suddenly, the richest man of his town came by in a sumptuous coach drawn by four horses, with two extra horses in the rear. When he saw the *melammed* trudging along with his bundle on his shoulders, he ordered his coachman to stop and asked: "Where are you going?"

The teacher told him.

"Well," said the rich man, "get into my carriage. I will take you there."

"Why not?" said the teacher.

To sit in the coach was a real pleasure; there was no lack of warm woolen blankets. Moreover,

[5] A teacher of children.

the rich man said to him: "Would you like some spirits?"

And so the *melammed* warmed himself with a bit of brandy and had a piece of cake with it. Then he took a piece of roast goose and another gulp of brandy. In brief, he felt quite in clover. Suddenly, he turned to the rich man: "Tell me, please, what are your worldly pleasures?"

The rich man looked at him with astonishment. "Don't you see? The coach and the horses, and the expensive food I can have even when traveling. Do you mean to say that all this is not enough worldly pleasure for a fellow like you?"

"No," said the *melammed* teasingly, "these are your heavenly pleasures, the acme of your pleasures, but where are your this-worldly pleasures?"

The perception of the spiritual, the experience of the wonder became common. Frequently, plain men began to feel what scholars had often failed to sense. And, indeed, does not the sigh of a contrite heart, or a bit of self-sacrifice outweigh the merits of him who is stuffed with both erudition and pride?

With many people, the attitude toward learning had become a kind of idolatry, depreciating the values of the heart. Excessive *pilpul* had often dried up the inner wells, and became the object of pretentious display of the intellect. Such self-indulgence, in the eyes of a Hasid, hurts more than sin. Opening a volume of the Talmud, he would sigh: "Lord of the world, perhaps I am among those of whom it is written: 'What right hast thou to proclaim my Laws?'" [6]

[6] Psalm 50:16.

"Love the Wicked"

HERE IS THE STORY OF A LEARNED MAN WHO CAME TO VISIT A REBBE. THE SCHOLAR WAS NO LONGER A YOUNG MAN —he was close to thirty—but he had never before visited a rebbe.

"What have you done all your life?" the master asked him.

"I have gone through the whole of the Talmud three times," answered the learned man.

"Yes, but how much of the Talmud has gone through you?" the rebbe inquired.

Out of sheer punctiliousness in observing the

law, one may come to be oblivious to the living presence of the Lord. But what is the main objective of observance, if not to feel the soul, the soul in oneself, in the Torah, in the world? Man is no mere reflection of the above—he is a spring. Divesting himself of the husks, he can illuminate the world. God has instilled in man something of Himself.

Israel, in particular, living for the "fulfillment of the Torah" is of unique importance. Hence, the fate of His beloved people of Israel is of such concern to God. God is the infinite, "the Hidden of all Hidden," whom no thought can conceive; but when a Jew has almost exhausted his strength in yearning after Him, he would exclaim: "Sweet Father!" It is incumbent upon us to obey our father in heaven, but God in turn is bound to take pity on his children. And his compassion is abundant, indeed. "I wish I could love the saintliest man in Israel as the Lord loves the most wicked in Israel," prayed Rabbi Aaron the Great. Yet, when the suffering of exile becomes too hard to bear and help from heaven fails to come, it is possible for Rabbi Levi Yitzhak of Berditshev [1] to summon God to stand trial, so to speak.

In 1917–1918, during the period of pogroms in Podolia, David Koigen,[2] engaged in recording

[1] A famous Hasidic leader.
[2] A philosopher and sociologist who died in 1933.

the events, was struck by the fact that in the various pogrom waves a certain town had been spared by the murderers. Other towns had been subjected to several pogroms, and here was a place which was situated in the path of the passing hordes and yet remained as though hidden from the hooligans.

One day, he happened to meet a resident from that town and asked him why it had been spared. The man said: "There is no reason to be surprised. We have a promise. Generations ago there lived in our town a great *zaddik*. It came to pass that on a certain Friday he had to go, for the sake of a *mitsvah*,[3] to a neighboring town. But he hesitated for a while. How set out on a journey on the day preceding the Sabbath? Delay on the road might prevent him from completing his journey before the advent of the Sabbath. But the matter was urgent, and it was possible to make the trip and return before sunset. So he went, fulfilled the *mitsvah*, and set out on his way home. The driver cracked his whip and the horses galloped. But the unforeseeable happened; the way grew longer and longer, and in the end, when the carriage entered his home town, the Sabbath candles were already gleaming from all Jewish homes. The *zaddik* was beside himself, he was wroth with the

[3] A commandment; the fulfillment of one's duty to God and man; a good deed.

Lord, that he had dealt in such a manner with him. In his indignation, he sternly refused to recite the Kiddush.[4] His refusal precipitated a great stir in heaven. But the *zaddik* would not forgive, not until he was assured that there would never be a pogrom in his town. Only then did he proceed to usher in the Sabbath."

The Baal Shem once spent the Seventh Day in a small village and stayed at an inn. When the Sabbath was about to end, the innkeeper called, as his custom was, all the Jews of the village together, in order to celebrate the Third Meal in their company with song and praise. "Why are you content to have the other Sabbath meals in the circle of your family, while for the Third Meal you look for the fellowship of many people?" asked the Baal Shem. And the innkeeper answered: "I understand that, in his last hour when a man is about to die, ten people should be present. With the passing of the Sabbath, the Additional Soul departs from us, and at the time of the Third Meal it is as if a part of us had passed away."

Purim, the joyous and merry festival commemorating the defeat of Haman's plot, was celebrated by some Hasidim in a spirit different in manner but identical in essence with the spirit

[4] The sanctification over wine and bread before the Friday evening meal.

that prevailed on the holiest of days, Yom ha-Kippurim, the Day of Atonement. Day after day, they performed the ritual of immersion in water, for without purification who would venture to engage upon a holy deed?

THIRTEEN

Thirty-Six Zaddikim

HE PRESENT MOMENT OVERFLOWED ITS
BOUNDS. PEOPLE LIVED NOT CHRONO-
LOGICALLY, BUT IN A FUSION OF PAST
and present. They lived with the great men of the
past, not only in narrating tales about them, but
also in their emotions and dreams. Jews studying
the Talmud felt a kinship with its sages. Elijah
the Prophet, it was believed, attended circum-
cision ceremonies, and the spirits of Holy Guests[1]

---

[1] According to the Zohar (III, 103b), when a man sits in
the *succah* (booth) "in the shadow of faith the Shekinah
spreads her wings over him from above," and the seven
holy guests "make their abode with him."

88

—Abraham, Isaac, Jacob, Moses, Aaron, Joseph, and David—visited their huts on the days of Sukkoth. Among such Jews, there lived the thirty-six Zaddikim[2] who remain unknown to the people and whose holiness sustains the universe. In their souls, simple Jews were always prepared to welcome the Messiah. If Isaiah the Prophet were to rise from his grave and were to enter the home of a Jew even on an ordinary Wednesday, the two would have understood each other.

Koretz, Karlin, Bratslav, Lubavich, Ger, Lublin—hundreds of little towns were like holy books. Each place was a pattern, an aspect, a way of Jewishness. When a Jew mentioned the name of a town like Miedzybosh or Berditshev, it was as though he mentioned a divine mystery. Supernatural splendor emanated from ordinary acts.

"Why do you go to see the rebbe?" someone asked an eminent rabbi who, although his time was precious, would trudge for days to visit his master on the Sabbath.

"To stand near him and watch him lace his shoes," he answered.

When Hasidim were gathered together, they told each other how the rebbe opened the door,

[2] The number of saintly men living in every generation for whose sake God extends his mercy to the world. They usually assume the guise of poor workmen so that their holiness remains unknown even to their intimates.

how he tasted of his food at the table—simple deeds, yet full of wonder.

What need was there to discuss faith? How was it possible not to feel the presence of God in the world? How could one fail to see that the whole earth is full of His glory? To preach to these Jews the necessity of observing the six hundred and thirteen commandments would have been superfluous. To live in accordance with the Shulhan Arukh had become second nature. But the Jews wanted more than that, they wanted to reach still higher levels. A leader of the Musar[3] movement once remarked: "If I thought that I should always remain what I am, I would lay hands on myself. But if I did not hope to be like the Gaon of Vilna,[4] I would not be even what I am." Such longing for the higher endowed them with an almost superhuman quality. Everyone knows what beauty is, everyone can perceive it with his senses. The new thing in Eastern Europe was that holiness, the highest of all values, became so real and so concrete that it became as perceptible as beauty.

Outwardly they were plagued by the misery and political humiliation which they had to en-

[3] An ethical movement initiated in the nineteenth century among the Jews of Lithuania by Rabbi Israel Salanter. For a beautiful portrait of Rabbi Salanter compare Ginzberg, Louis, Students, Scholars and Saints, pp. 145-194.
[4] The greatest talmudic scholar of his time (1720-1797).

dure, but inwardly they bore the rich sorrow of the world and the noble vision of redemption for all men and all beings. There were Jews from whose spirit the suffering of past ages and of their own time never departed. Yet, this did not disturb the flow of their daily festive faith. For man is not alone in the world. "Despair does not exist at all," said Rabbi Nahman of Bratslav, a Hasidic leader. "Do not fear, dear child, God is with you, in you, around you. Even in the Nethermost Pit one can try to come closer to God." The word "bad" never came to their lips. Disasters did not frighten them. "You can take everything from me—the pillow from under my head, my house— but you cannot take God from my heart."

Miracles no longer startled anyone, and it was no surprise to discover among one's contemporaries men who attained the holy spirit, men whose ear perceived the voice of heaven. People ceased to think that their generation was inferior to the earlier; they no longer considered themselves epigones. On the contrary, Hasidim believed that it was easier to attain inspiration by the Holy Spirit in their own day than it had been in the early days of the Talmud. For such inspiration flows from two sources—from the Temple in Jerusalem and from the Complete Redemption in the time of the Messiah. And we are closer to the time of Redemption than the Talmudic sages were to the era of the Temple. The light of the Messiah can already be seen before us, illuminating contemporary holy men. "One has to be blind not to see the light of the Messiah," said Rabbi Pinhas of Koretz. He felt pity for Rabbi Abraham Ibn Ezra of the eleventh century, whose period was distant both from the sources of prophecy at the time of the Temple and from the light of the Messiah's era. That explained why he was so sober, why he was unable to appreciate the hidden depth of the inspired hymns of Rabbi Eleazar Hakalir.

The feeling prevailed that man was superior to angels; the angel knows no self-sacrifice, does not have to overcome obstacles, has no free choice in his actions. Moreover, the nature of an angel is stationary, keeping forever the rank in which he was created. Man, however, is a wayfarer, he always moves either upward or downward; he cannot remain in one place. More than that. Man is not only the crown of creation, he can become a participant in the act of creation. The Hasidim realized the wide range of their responsibility, they knew that entire worlds waited to be redeemed from imperfection. Not only are we in need of heaven, but heaven needs us as well.

The little Jewish communities in Eastern Europe were like sacred texts opened before the eyes of God so close were their houses of worship to Mount Sinai. In the humble wooden synagogues, looking as if they were deliberately closing themselves off from the world, the Jews purified the souls that God had given them and perfected their likeness to God. There arose in them an infinite world of inwardness, a "Torah within the Heart," beside the written and oral Torah. Even plain men were like artists who knew how to fill weekday hours with mystic beauty. They did not write songs, they themselves were songs. When Jews stood prepared to receive the "Additional Sabbath Soul" and once again fell in love with God, reciting the portion of the Book of Splendor on "the mystery of the Sabbath," they reached heights of beauty and ecstasy. They often lacked outward brilliance, but they were full of hidden light.

To the wisest among them, it was more important to fulfill what they said than to say what they fulfilled.

In the spiritual dimension, self-renunciation counts more than achievement of scholarship. Rabbi Isaac Meir Alter of Ger, the outstanding Talmudic scholar in Poland of his day, came to his master, Rabbi Mendel of Kotzk, and asked him to read the manuscript of a work he had written. It was a commentary on Hoshen Mishpat, the Jewish Civil Code. A few weeks later, the rabbi of Kotzk sent for the author. "I have studied your manuscript," he said. "It is a work of genius. When published, the classical commentaries, which have been studied for generations, will become obsolete. I am only grieved at the thought of the displeasure which this will cause to the souls of the saintly commentators." It was a winter evening. Fire was burning in the stove. Rabbi Isaac Meir took the manuscript from the table and threw it into the flames.

"Guard My Tongue from Evil"

IT WAS NOT BY ACCIDENT THAT THE JEWS OF EASTERN EUROPE THOUGHT LITTLE OF WORLDLY EDUCATION. THEY RESISTED the stream of enlightenment which threatened to engulf the small province of Jewishness. They did not despise science. They believed, however, that a bit of spiritual nobility was a thousand times more valuable than all the secular sciences, that praying three times a day "My God, guard my tongue from evil" was more important than the study of physics, that meditating upon the

95

Psalms filled man with more compassion than the study of Roman history.

They put no trust in the secular world. They believed that the existence of the world was not contingent on museums and libraries, but on houses of worship and study. To them, the house of study was not important because the world needed it, but, on the contrary, the world was important because houses of study existed in it. To them, life without the Torah and without piety was chaos, and a man who lived without these was looked upon with a sense of fear. They realized quite well that the world was full of ordeals and dangers, that it contained Cain's jealousy of Abel, the cold malevolence of Sodom, and the hatred of Esau, but they also knew that there was in it the charity of Abraham and the tenderness of Rachel.

Harassed and oppressed, they carried deep within their hearts a contempt for the "world," with its power and pomp, with its bustling and boasting. People who at midnight lamented the glory of God that is in exile and spent their days peddling onions were not insulted by the scorn of their enemies nor impressed by their praises. They knew that the Jews were in exile, that the world was unredeemed. Their life was oriented to the spiritual, and they could therefore ignore its external aspects. Outwardly a Jew might have been a pauper, but inwardly he felt like a prince, a kin to the king of kings. Unconquerable freedom was in him who, when wrapped in *tallith* and *tefillin*, consecrated his soul to the sanctification of the Holy Name.

There are more attractive literatures and subtler philosophies than those created by the East European Jews, but in the figures and ideas of the latter, the light of the likeness to God was never extinguished. There were Jews who claimed that they could recall how their souls witnessed the Revelation at Mount Sinai. From their souls came the constant cry, "We will do and we will listen," and rarely was this affirmation uttered more sincerely. Fiery young men would break into the streets and proclaim: "There is none beside Him!"

Has there ever been more light in the souls of the Jews in the last thousand years? Could it have been more beautiful in Safed or in Worms, in Cordoba or Pumbeditha?

The Jews had always known piety and Sabbath holiness. The new thing in Eastern Europe was that somewhat of the Sabbath was infused into every day. One could relish the taste of life eternal in the fleeting moment. In such an environment, it was not difficult to maintain the *neshama yetherah*, the Additional Soul, which every Jew is given for the day of Sabbath. There were no concerts or operas in their little towns; yet what

97

they felt when attending the Third Sabbath Meal, no songs were eloquent enough to express. Jews did not build magnificent synagogues; they built bridges leading from the heart to God.

The story is told that once the holy Baal Shem and his disciples came to Berditshev to see Rabbi Lieber the Great. Rabbi Lieber was not at home. It was the day of the fair; so the visitors went to the market, and there they saw Rabbi Lieber conversing with a peasant. "Do you know with whom Rabbi Lieber is speaking?" the Baal Shem asked his disciples. "It is Elijah the Prophet." Beholding the amazement of the disciples, he added: "It is not Rabbi Lieber who is privileged to have a revelation of Elijah, but Elijah who is privileged to have a revelation of Rabbi Lieber."

This story perhaps best expresses what happened in that period. In the days of Moses, Israel had a revelation of God, in the days of the Baal Shem, God had a revelation of Israel. Suddenly, there was revealed a holiness in Jewish life that had accumulated in the course of many generations. Ultimately, the "We will do and we will listen" [1] is as important as the "I am the Lord thy God." [2] And "Who is like thy people Israel, a nation, unique in the earth" [3] is as meaningful to

[1] Exodus 24:7.   [2] Exodus 20:2.   [3] II Samuel 7:23.

Him as "The Lord is One"[4] is to Israel. "Who would have believed our report? And to whom hath the arm of the Lord been revealed?"[5] One looked at the Jews and perceived the Shekinah.

When Nebuchadnezzar destroyed Jerusalem and set fire to the Temple, our forefathers did not forget the Revelation at Mount Sinai and the words of the Prophets. Today the world knows that what transpired on the soil of Palestine was sacred history, from which mankind draws inspiration. A day may come when the hidden light of the East European era may be revealed.

[4] Deuteronomy 6:4.   [5] Isaiah 53:1.

The Untold Story

TO BE SURE, IN THE LIFE OF THE EAST EUROPEAN JEWS THERE WAS NOT ONLY LIGHT BUT ALSO SHADOW—ONE-SIDEDness of learning, neglect of manners, provincialism. In the crowded conditions in which they lived—persecuted and tormented by ruthless laws, intimidated by drunken landowners, despised by newly enriched city dwellers, trampled by police boots, chosen as scapegoats by political demagogues—the rope of discipline sometimes snapped. In addition, naked misery and frightful poverty deafened the demands and admonitions of religious enthusiasm. The regions of piety were at times too lofty for plain mortals.

Not all the Jews could devote themselves to the Torah and service to God, not all of their old men had the faces of prophets; there were not only Hasidim and Kabbalists, but also yokels and tramps. But even in the mud of their little towns there were pearling, tender flowers, and in the darkness, sparks smoldered waiting to be kindled.

There was hardly a Jew in whom respect for the spirit had died out completely. There were always moralists who publicly branded the abuses that arose in the Jewish communities and hurled flaming denunciations at those who sat above, unconcerned with justice. The faults were in the limelight; *schnorrers* spread far and wide the knowledge of their unsavory qualities.

The record of quiet self-sacrifice, of unpublicized charity, of inwardness and devotion of the plain folk, of those who patiently bore their poverty and did not run abroad to seek their fortune will probably remain forever untold.

It is easier to appraise the beauty of traditional Jewish life than the revolutionary spirituality of the modern Jews. The Jew of older days often overlooked this world because of his preference for the other world. Between man and world stood God. In the meantime, however, persecutions, pogroms, and murders shattered the ground under the feet of the people. There was no peace, no security, and the means to gain a livelihood were systematically taken away. The Slavonic masses, dominated by self-complacent landowners, feebly responded to the impulses of the industrial revolution that swept through the northern countries in the nineteenth century. Lacking the drive to enterprise, landowners, civil service, and peasantry alike ignored the challenge of the shaking transformation. The average man preferred to live on the public pay roll as a state or municipal official rather than to be exposed to the risks of free commerce. As a result of failure to exploit natural resources and to substitute modern for antiquated methods in farming and trade, the people lived in misery and poverty. The increasing pauperization affected particularly the Jewish population, engaged to some extent in agriculture, but mainly in handicraft and trade, which for want of capital and because of systematic oppression by the state had scarcely any hope of recovery. Pioneers in city building and in developing important industries, the Jews encountered a mounting well-planned system of curbs and obstacles. Jewish youth, restless, alert, and flexible, eager and full of dynamic impulses, looked for a way out of the gloomy and overcrowded streets, where no chance of improvement, no conditions for development could be found.

Then came young men with new tidings; they refused to accept misfortune passively, they wanted to build their existence on their own soil. They no longer wanted to live on miracles, they wanted freedom, a natural way of life. They did not want to live spiritually off the past; they refused to live on bequests; they wanted to begin anew.

The cosmopolitan breeze of enlightenment blowing from the West with its optimistic message of emancipation for all people brought a flash of hope into the Jewish communities. The romanticism of poets and students, aspiring to bring about a revival of the Hebrew language, concurred with the post-Mendelssohnian activities aiming at rationalizing and unraveling the contents of Jewish life and lore. There arose the Enlightenment movement (Haskalah), Zionism, the Halutzim movement, Jewish socialism. How much of self-sacrifice, of love for the people, of Sanctification of the Holy Name are to be found in the modern Jews, in their will to suffer in order to help! The zeal of the pious Jews was transferred to their emancipated sons and grandsons. The fervor and yearning of the Hasidim, the ascetic obstinacy of the Kabbalists, the inexorable logic of the Talmudists, were reincarnated in the supporters of modern Jewish movements. Their belief in new ideals was infused with age-old piety. They could see a "daughter of heaven" in the message of rationalism, a holy temple in the revived Hebrew language or the essence of Judaism in Yiddish, the "mother tongue."

They believed in Europe and extolled the "twentieth century." To absorb the culture and ideas of Western civilization was their passionate desire, their dream of happiness. Yet, unlike the ancient sects, even those who felt that for the sake of adopting the modern they had to abandon the old, even those whom the revolutionary impetus had carried to the antithesis of tradition, have not severed the ties from the people; with few exceptions, they have remained within the fold. The powerful urge to redemption survived in their souls. The allurements of assimilation were, indeed, seductive; but the Jews who did not capitulate, who did not flee from Jewish poverty, who gave up careers, comfort, and fame, in order to find healing for the hurt of their people, who left the sacred books or the universities to till the ground and dry the swamps of Palestine, were like old wine in new bottles.

The masses of East European Jews repudiated emancipation when it was offered at the price of disloyalty to Israel's traditions. Both pious and freethinking Jews fought for a dignified existence, striving to assure the rights of the community, not only those of the individual. They manifested a collective will for a collective aim. With lightning rapidity, they straightened their backs and learned to master the arts and sciences. Gifts for abstract dialectical thinking, developed in the course of generations, were carried into scientific research. Hasidic enthusiasm was sublimated in the noble profundity of musical virtuosos. Three thousand years of history have not made them weary. Their spirits were animated by a vitality that often drove them into opposition to accepted tenets.

In the spiritual confusion of the last hundred years, many of us overlooked the incomparable beauty of our old, poor homes. We compared our fathers and grandfathers, our scholars and rabbis, with Russian or German intellectuals. We preached in the name of the twentieth century, measured the merits of Berditshev and Ger with the standards of Paris and Heidelberg. Dazzled by the lights of the metropolis, we lost at times the inner sight. The luminous visions that for so many generations shone in the little candles were extinguished for some of us.

In the last decades, there has developed a longing for an accord between the present and the past. The antithesis of the Haskalah had gradually begun to change into a synthesis. Gradually the inner beauty of the old life and the emptiness of present-day civilization have been disclosed. But the time has been too short and the will too weak. Clarity and solidarity have been lacking not only in spiritual but also in political matters. When confronted with a world of misery and indifference, our will and our vision proved inadequate. In our zeal to change, in our passion to advance, we ridiculed superstition until we lost our ability to believe. We have helped to extinguish the light our fathers had kindled. We have bartered holiness for convenience, loyalty for success, wisdom for information, prayers for sermons, tradition for fashion.

In the elementary textbooks of Hebrew in use a quarter of a century ago, there was a story of a schoolboy who would be in great distress every morning, having forgotten where he put away his clothes and books before he went to bed. One evening he arrived at an answer to his problem. He wrote on a slip of paper: "The suit is on the chair, the hat is in the closet, the books on the desk, the shoes under the chair, and I am in bed." Next morning he began to collect his things together. They were all in their places. When he came to the last item on the list, he went to look for himself in the bed—but his search was in vain.

A world has vanished. All that remains is a sanctuary hidden in the realm of spirit. We of this generation are still holding the key. Unless we remember, unless we unlock it, the holiness of ages will remain a secret of God. We of this generation are still holding the key—the key to the sanctuary which is also the shelter of our own deserted souls. If we mislay the key, we shall elude ourselves.

In this hour we, the living, are "the people of Israel." The tasks, begun by the patriarchs and prophets and continued by their descendants, are now entrusted to us. We are either the last Jews or those who will hand over the entire past to generations to come. We will either forfeit or enrich the legacy of ages.

Judaism today is the least known religion. Its rare splendor has been so frequently adjusted to the trivialities of changing opinions that what is left is a commonplace. There are only few who still perceive the vanishing *niggun* of its perennial yearning.

Mankind does not have the choice of religion and neutrality. Irreligion is not opiate but poison. Our energies are too abundant for living indifferently. We are in need of an endless purpose to absorb our immense power if our souls are not to run amok. We are either the ministers of the sacred or slaves of evil. To be a Jew is to hold one's soul clean and open the stream of endless striving so that God may not be ashamed of His creation. Judaism is not a quality of the soul but spiritual life. With souls we are born; spirit we must acquire.

Judaism is the track of God in the wilderness of oblivion. By being what we are, namely Jews; by attuning our own yearning to the lonely holiness in this world, we will aid humanity more than by any particular service we may render.

We are Jews as we are men. The alternative to our Jewish existence is spiritual suicide, disappearance, not conversion into something else. Judaism has allies, partners, but no substitute. It is not a handmaiden of civilization but its touchstone.

We do not live in a void. We never suffer from a fear of roaming about in the emptiness of Time. We own the past and are, hence, not afraid of what is to be. We remember where we came from. We are endowed with the consciousness of being involved in a history that transcends the interests and glories of particular dynasties and empires. We were summoned and cannot forget it, winding the clock of eternal history. We are taught to feel the knots of life in which the trivial is intertwined with the sublime. There is no end to our experience of the intense, stern import, of the dangerous grandeur, of the divine earnestness of human life. Our blossoms may be crushed, but we are upheld by the faith that comes from beneath our roots.

Our life is beset with difficulties, yet it is never devoid of meaning. The feeling of futility is absent from our souls. Our existence is not in vain. There is a Divine earnestness about our life. This is our dignity. To be invested with dignity means to represent something more than oneself. The gravest sin for a Jew is to forget what he represents.

We are God's stake in human history. We are the dawn and the dusk, the challenge and the test. How strange to be a Jew and to go astray on God's perilous errands. We have been offered as a pattern of worship and as a prey for scorn, but there is more still in our destiny. We carry the gold of God in our souls to forge the gate of the kingdom. The time for the kingdom may be far off, but the task is plain: to retain our share in God in spite of peril and contempt. There is a war to wage against the vulgar, against the glorification of the absurd, a war that is incessant, universal. Loyal to the presence of the ultimate in the common, we may be able to make it clear that man is more than man, that in doing the finite he may perceive the infinite.

About
JEWISH LIGHTS Publishing

P eople of all faiths and backgrounds yearn for books
that attract, engage, educate and spiritually inspire.

Our principal goal is to stimulate thought and help all
people learn about who the Jewish People are, where
they come from, and what the future can be made to
hold. While people of our diverse Jewish heritage are
the primary audience, our books speak to people in the
Christian world as well and will broaden their understanding of Judaism and the roots of their own faith.

We bring to you authors who are at the forefront of
spiritual thought and experience. While each has
something different to say, they all say it in a voice that
you can hear.

Our books are designed to welcome you and then to
engage, stimulate and inspire. We judge our success
not only by whether or not our books are beautiful and
commercially successful, but by whether or not they
make a difference in your life.

We at Jewish Lights take great care to produce beautiful
books that present meaningful spiritual content in a
form that reflects the art of making high quality books.

Theology/Philosophy

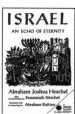

ISRAEL
An Echo of Eternity
by *Abraham Joshua Heschel* with New Introduction by *Susannah Heschel*

In this classic reprint originally published by Farrar, Straus & Giroux, one of the foremost religious figures of our century gives us a powerful and eloquent statement on the meaning of Israel in our time. Heschel looks at the past, present and future home of the Jewish people. He tells us how and why the presence of Israel has tremendous historical and religious significance for the whole world.

5 1/2 x 8, 272 pp. Quality Paperback Original, ISBN 1-879045-70-2 **$18.95**

THE SPIRIT OF RENEWAL
Finding Faith After the Holocaust
by *Edward Feld*

"Boldly redefines the landscape of Jewish religious thought after the Holocaust."
—*Rabbi Lawrence Kushner*

Trying to understand the Holocaust and addressing the question of faith after the Holocaust, Rabbi Feld explores three key cycles of destruction and recovery in Jewish history, each of which radically reshaped Jewish understanding of God, people, and the world.

• AWARD WINNER •

"A profound meditation on Jewish history [and the Holocaust]....Christians, as well as many others, need to share in this story."
—*The Rt. Rev. Frederick H. Borsch, Ph.D., Episcopal Bishop of L.A.*

6" x 9", 224 pp. Quality Paperback, ISBN 1-879045-40-0 **$16.95** HC, ISBN-06-0 **$22.95**

SEEKING THE PATH TO LIFE
Theological Meditations On God
and the Nature of People, Love, Life and Death
by *Rabbi Ira F. Stone*

For people who never thought they would read a book of theology—let alone understand it, enjoy it, savor it and have it affect the way they think about their lives. In 45 intense meditations, each a page or two in length, Stone takes us on explorations of the most basic human struggles: Life and death, love and anger, peace and war, covenant and exile.

• AWARD WINNER • "A bold book....The reader of any faith will be inspired...."
— *The Rev. Carla V. Berkedal, Episcopal Priest*

6" x 9", 132 pp. Quality Paperback, ISBN 1-879045-47-8 **$14.95** HC, ISBN-17-6 **$19.95**

THEOLOGY & PHILOSOPHY...Other books—Classic Reprints

Tormented Master: The Life and Spiritual Quest of Rabbi Nahman of Bratslav
by Arthur Green

6 x 9, 408 pp, Quality Paperback, ISBN 1-879045-11-7 **$18.95**

The Earth Is the Lord's: The Inner World of the Jew in Eastern Europe
by Abraham Joshua Heschel with woodcut illustrations by Ilya Schor

5 1/2 x 8, 112 pp, Quality Paperback, ISBN 1-879045-42-7 **$13.95**

A Passion for Truth by Abraham Joshua Heschel

5 1/2 x 8, 352 pp, Quality Paperback, ISBN 1-879045-41-9 **$18.95**

Your Word Is Fire
Edited and translated with a new introduction by Arthur Green and Barry W. Holtz

6 x 9, 152 pp, Quality Paperback, ISBN 1-879045-25-7 **$14.95**

Aspects of Rabbinic Theology
by Solomon Schechter, with a New Introduction by Neil Gillman

6 x 9, 440 pp, Quality Paperback, ISBN 1-879045-24-9 **$18.95**

The Last Trial: On the Legends and Lore of the Command to Abraham to Offer Isaac as a Sacrifice by Shalom Spiegel, with a new introduction by Judah Goldin

6 x 9, 208 pp, Quality Paperback, ISBN 1-879045-29-X **$17.95**

Spirituality—The Kushner Series

INVISIBLE LINES OF CONNECTION
Sacred Stories of the Ordinary
by *Lawrence Kushner*

Through his everyday encounters with family, friends, colleagues and strangers, Kushner takes us deeply into our lives, finding flashes of spiritual insight in the process. This is a book where literature meets spirituality, where the sacred meets the ordinary, and, above all, where people of all faiths, all backgrounds can meet one another and themselves.

"Does something both more and different than instruct—it inspires. Wonderful stories, from the best storyteller I know."
— *David Mamet*

5 1/2" x 8.5", 160 pp. Hardcover, ISBN 1-879045-52-4 **$21.95**

HONEY FROM THE ROCK
An Easy Introduction to Jewish Mysticism

'Quite simply the easiest introduction to Jewish mysticism you can read."

n introduction to the ten gates of Jewish mysticism and how it applies to ily life.

"Captures the flavor and spark of Jewish mysticism. . . . Read it and be rewarded."
—*Elie Wiesel*

6" x 9", 168 pp. Quality Paperback, ISBN 1-879045-02-8 **$14.95**

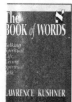

THE BOOK OF WORDS
Talking Spiritual Life, Living Spiritual Talk
by *Lawrence Kushner*

In the incomparable manner of his extraordinary *The Book of Letters*, Kushner now lifts up and shakes the dust off primary religious words we use to describe the spiritual dimension of life. For each word Kushner offers us a startling, moving and insightful explication, and pointed readings from classical Jewish sources that further illuminate the concept. He concludes with a short exercise that helps unite the spirit of the word with our actions in the world.

This is a powerful and holy book."
—*M. Scott Peck, M.D., author of* The Road Less Traveled *and other books*

What a delightful wholeness of intellectual vigor and meditative playfulness, and all in tone of gentleness that speaks to this gentile."
—*Rt. Rev. Krister Stendahl, formerly Dean, Harvard Divinity School/Bishop of Stockholm*

6" x 9", 152 pp. Hardcover, beautiful two-color text ISBN 1-879045-35-4 **$21.95**

THE BOOK OF LETTERS
A Mystical Hebrew Alphabet
by *Rabbi Lawrence Kushner*

calligraphy by the author. Folktales about and exploration of the mystical meangs of the Hebrew Alphabet. Open the old prayerbook-like pages of *The Book of etters* and you will enter a special world of sacred tradition and religious feeling. abbi Kushner draws from ancient Judaic sources, weaving Talmudic commenry, Hasidic folktales, and Kabbalistic mysteries around the letters.

A book which is in love with Jewish letters."
— *Isaac Bashevis Singer* (לז)

Popular Hardcover Edition 6"x 9", 80 pp. Hardcover, two colors, inspiring new reword. ISBN 1-879045-00-1 **$24.95**

Deluxe Gift Edition 9"x 12", 80 pp. Hardcover, four-color text, ornamentation, in a beautiful slipcase. BN 1-879045-01-X **$79.95**

Collector's Limited Edition 9"x 12", 80 pp. Hardcover, gold embossed pages, hand assembled slipcase. With kscreened print. **Limited to 500 signed and numbered copies.** ISBN 1-879045-04-4 **$349.00**

To see a sample page at no obligation, call us

Spirituality

GOD WAS IN THIS PLACE & I, i DID NOT KNOW
Finding Self, Spirituality & Ultimate Meaning
by Lawrence Kushner

Who am I? Who is God? Kushner creates inspiring interpretations of Jacob's dream in Genesis, opening a window into Jewish spirituality for people of all faiths and backgrounds.

In this fascinating blend of scholarship, imagination, psychology and history, seven Jewish spiritual masters ask and answer fundamental questions of human experience.

"Rich and intriguing."
—*M. Scott Peck, M.D., author of* The Road Less Traveled *and other books*

6" x 9", 192 pp. Quality Paperback, ISBN 1-879045-33-8 **$16.95** HC, ISBN -05-2 **$21.95**

THE RIVER OF LIGHT
Spirituality, Judaism, Consciousness
by Lawrence Kushner

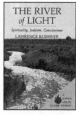

"manual" for all spiritual travelers who would attempt a spiritual journey in ır times. Taking us step by step, Kushner allows us to discover the meaning of ır own quest: "to allow the river of light—the deepest currents of conscious-ıss—to rise to the surface and animate our lives."

>hilosophy and mystical fantasy....Anybody—Jewish, Christian, or other-ise...will find this book an intriguing experience."
—*The Kirkus Reviews*

6" x 9", 180 pp. Quality Paperback, ISBN 1-879045-03-6 **$14.95**

SELF, STRUGGLE & CHANGE
Family Conflict Stories in Genesis
and Their Healing Insights for Our Lives
by Norman J. Cohen

How do I find greater wholeness in my life and in my family's life?

The stress of late-20th-century living only brings new variations to timeless personal struggles. The people described in Genesis were in situations and relationships very much like our own. Their stories still speak to us because they are about the same problems *we* deal with every day. A modern master of biblical interpreta-tion brings us greater understanding of the ancient text and of ourselves in this intriguing re-telling conflict between husband and wife, father and son, brothers, and sisters.

"A delightful and instructive book; recommended."
—*Library Journal*

6" x 9", 224 pp. Quality Paperback, ISBN 1-879045-66-4 **$16.95** HC, ISBN -19-2 **$21.95**

BEING GOD'S PARTNER
How to Find the Hidden Link Between
Spirituality and Your Work
by Jeffrey K. Salkin Introduction by *Norman Lear*

book that will challenge people of every denomination to reconcile the cares of ork and soul. A groundbreaking book about spirituality and the work world, om a Jewish perspective. Helps the reader find God in the ethical striving and arch for meaning in the professions and in business and offers practical sugges-ıns for balancing your professional life and spiritual self.

his engaging meditation on the spirituality of work is grounded in Judaism t is relevant well beyond the boundaries of that tradition."
—*Booklist (American Library Association)*

6" x 9", 192 pp. Quality Paperback, ISBN 1-879045-65-6 **$16.95,** HC, ISBN -37-0 **$19.95**

Spirituality

HOW TO BE A PERFECT STRANGER, In 2 Volumes
A Guide to Etiquette in Other People's
Religious Ceremonies
Edited by Stuart M. Matlins & Arthur J. Magida

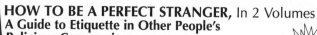
BEST
REFERENCE
BOOK OF
THE YEAR

"A book that belongs in every living room, library and office!"

Explains the rituals and celebrations of America's major religions/denominations, helping an interested guest to feel comfortable, participate to the fullest extent possible, and avoid violating anyone's religious principles. Answers practical questions from the perspective of *any* other faith.

VOL. 1: America's Largest Faiths

VOL. 1 COVERS: Assemblies of God • Baptist • Buddhist • Christian Science • Churches of Christ • Disciples of Christ • Episcopalian • Greek Orthodox • Hindu • Islam • Jehovah's Witnesses • Jewish • Lutheran • Methodist • Mormon • Presbyterian • Quaker • Roman Catholic • Seventh-day Adventist • United Church of Christ

6" x 9", 432 pp. Hardcover, ISBN 1-879045-39-7 **$24.95**

VOL. 2: Other Faiths in America

VOL. 2 COVERS: African American Methodist Churches • Baha'i • Christian and Missionary Alliance • Christian Congregation • Church of the Brethren • Church of the Nazarene • Evangelical Free Church of America • International Church of the Foursquare Gospel • International Pentecostal Holiness Church • Mennonite/Amish • Native American • Orthodox Churches • Pentecostal Church of God • Reformed Church of America • Sikh • Unitarian Universalist • Wesleyan

6" x 9", 416 pp. Hardcover, ISBN 1-879045-63-X **$24.95**

GOD & THE BIG BANG
Discovering Harmony Between Science & Spirituality
by *Daniel C. Matt*

Mysticism and science: What do they have in common? How can one enlighten the other? By drawing on modern cosmology and ancient Kabbalah, Matt shows how science and religion can together enrich our spiritual awareness and help us recover a sense of wonder and find our place in the universe.

"This poetic new book...helps us to understand the human meaning of creation."
—*Joel Primack, leading cosmologist, Professor of Physics, University of California, Santa Cruz*

6" x 9", 216 pp. Hardcover, ISBN 1-879045-48-6 **$21.95**

MINDING THE TEMPLE OF THE SOUL
Balancing Body, Mind & Spirit through Traditional Jewish Prayer, Movement & Meditation
by *Tamar Frankiel* and *Judy Greenfeld*

This new spiritual approach to physical health introduces readers to a spiritual tradition that affirms the body and enables them to reconceive their bodies in a more positive light. Relying on Kabbalistic teachings and other Jewish traditions, it shows us how to be more responsible for our own psychological and physical health. Focuses on the discipline of prayer, simple Tai Chi-like exercises and body positions, and guides the reader throughout, step by step, with diagrams, sketches and meditations.

7 x 10, 184 pp, Quality Paperback Original, illus., ISBN 1-879045-64-8 **$15.95**

Audiotape of the Prayers, Movements & Meditations (60-min. cassette) **$9.95**

Spirituality

THE EMPTY CHAIR: FINDING HOPE & JOY
Timeless Wisdom from a Hasidic Master, Rebbe Nachman of Breslov
Adapted by *Moshe Mykoff* and *The Breslov Research Institute*

A "little treasure" of aphorisms and advice for living joyously and spiritually today, written 200 years ago, but startlingly fresh in meaning and use. Challenges and helps us to move from stress and sadness to hope and joy.

Teacher, guide and spiritual master—Rebbe Nachman provides vital words of inspiration and wisdom for life today for people of any faith, or of no faith.

"For anyone of any faith, this is a book of healing and wholeness, of being alive!"
—*Bookviews*

4" x 6", 128 pp. Deluxe Paperback, 2-color text, ISBN 1-879045-67-2 **$9.95**

FINDING JOY
A Practical Spiritual Guide to Happiness
by *Dannel I. Schwartz* with *Mark Hass*

arching for happiness in our modern world of stress and struggle is common; *ding* it is more unusual. This guide explores and explains how to find joy rough a time-honored, creative—and surprisingly practical—approach based on e teachings of Jewish mysticism and Kabbalah.

his lovely, simple introduction to Kabbalah....is a singular contribution to *kun olam*, repairing the world."
—*American Library Association's* Booklist

•AWARD WINNER•

6" x 9", 192 pp. Hardcover, ISBN 1-879045-53-2 **$19.95**

THE DEATH OF DEATH
Resurrection and Immortality in Jewish Thought
by *Neil Gillman*

Noted theologian Neil Gillman explores the original and compelling argument that Judaism, a religion often thought to pay little attention to the afterlife, not only offers us rich ideas on the subject—but delivers a deathblow to death itself. By exploring Jewish thought about death and the afterlife, this fascinating work presents us with challenging new ideas about our lives.

nables us to recover our tradition's understanding of the afterlife and breaks through the silence modern Jewish thought on immortality.... A work of major significance."
—*Rabbi Sheldon Zimmerman, President, Hebrew Union College–Jewish Institute of Religion*

6" x 9", 336 pp, Hardcover, ISBN 1-879045-61-3 **$23.95**

GODWRESTLING—ROUND 2
Ancient Wisdom, Future Paths
by *Arthur Waskow*

BEST RELIGION BOOK OF THE YEAR

This 20th anniversary sequel to a seminal book of the Jewish renewal movement deals with spirituality in relation personal growth, marriage, ecology, feminism, politics, and more. Including v chapters on recent issues and concerns, Waskow outlines original ways to rge "religious" life and "personal" life in our society today.

• Award Winner •

"A delicious read and a soaring meditation."
—*Rabbi Zalman M. Schachter-Shalomi*

6" x 9", 352 pp. Hardcover, ISBN 1-879045-45-1 **$23.95**

Healing/Recovery/Wellness

Experts Praise *Twelve Jewish Steps to Recovery*

"Recommended reading for people of all denominations."
—*Rabbi Abraham J. Twerski, M.D.*

TWELVE JEWISH STEPS TO RECOVERY
A Personal Guide To Turning From Alcoholism & Other Addictions...Drugs, Food, Gambling, Sex
by *Rabbi Kerry M. Olitzky* & *Stuart A. Copans, M.D.*
Preface by *Abraham J. Twerski, M.D.*; Intro. by *Rabbi Sheldon Zimmerman* "Getting Help" by *JACS Foundation*

A Jewish perspective on the Twelve Steps of addiction recovery programs with consolation, inspiration and motivation for recovery. It draws from traditional sources and quotes from what recovering Jewish people say about their experiences with addictions of all kinds. Inspiring illustrations of the twelve gates of the Old City of Jerusalem.

6" x 9", 136 pp. Quality Paperback, ISBN 1-879045-09-5 **$13.95**   HC, ISBN -08-7 **$19.95**

Recovery from Codependence: A Jewish Twelve Steps Guide to Healing Your Soul
by Dr. Kerry M. Olitzky

6" x 9", 160 pp. Quality Paperback Original, ISBN 1-879045-32-X **$13.95**   HC, ISBN -27-3 **$21.95**

Renewed Each Day: Daily Twelve Step Recovery Meditations Based on the Bible
by Dr. Kerry M. Olitzky & Aaron Z.

6" x 9", Quality Paperback Original,   **V. I**, 224 pp. **$12.95**   **V. II**, 280 pp. **$14.95**
Two-Volume Set ISBN 1-879045-21-4   **$27.90**

One Hundred Blessings Every Day: Daily Twelve Step Recovery Affirmations, Exercises for Personal Growth & Renewal Reflecting Seasons of the Jewish Year
by Dr. Kerry M. Olitzky

4 1/2" x 6 1/2", 432 pp. Quality Paperback Original, ISBN 1-879045-30-3 **$14.95**

HEALING OF SOUL, HEALING OF BODY
Spiritual Leaders Unfold the Strength and Solace in Psalms
Edited by *Rabbi Simkha Y. Weintraub, CSW, for The Jewish Healing Center*

A source of solace for those who are facing illness, as well as those who care for them. The ten Psalms which form the core of this healing resource were originally selected 200 years ago by Rabbi Nachman of Breslov as a "complete remedy." Today, for anyone coping with illness, they continue to provide a wellspring of strength. Each Psalm is newly translated, making it clear and accessible, and each one is introduced by an eminent rabbi, men and women reflecting different movements and backgrounds. To all who are living with the pain and uncertainty of illness, this spiritual resource offers an anchor of spiritual comfort.

"Will bring comfort to anyone fortunate enough to read it. This gentle book is a luminous gem of wisdom."
—*Larry Dossey, M.D., author of* Healing Words: The Power of Prayer & the Practice of Medicine

6" x 9", 128 pp. Quality Paperback Original, illus., 2-color text, ISBN 1-879045-31-1 **$14.95**

Life Cycle

THE NEW JEWISH BABY BOOK
Names, Ceremonies, Customs—A Guide for Today's Families
by *Anita Diamant*

A complete guide to the customs and rituals for welcoming a new child to the world and into the Jewish community, and for commemorating this joyous event in family life—whatever your family constellation. Includes new ceremonies for girls, celebrations in interfaith families, and more.

"A book that all Jewish parents—no matter how religious—will find fascinating as well as useful. It is a perfect shower or new baby gift."
— *Pamela Abrams, Exec. Editor,* Parents Magazine

6" x 9", 328 pp. Quality Paperback Original, ISBN 1-879045-28-1 **$16.95**

PUTTING GOD ON THE GUEST LIST, 2ND ED.
How to Reclaim the Spiritual Meaning of Your Child's Bar or Bat Mitzvah
by *Rabbi Jeffrey K. Salkin*

BEST RELIGION BOOK OF THE YEAR

Joining explanation, instruction and inspiration, helps parent and child truly *be there* when the moment of Sinai is recreated in their lives. Asks and answers such fundamental questions as how did Bar and Bat Mitzvah originate? What the lasting significance of the event? How to make the event more spiritually meaningful? New 2nd Edition.

New! 2nd Ed.

"I hope every family planning a Bar Mitzvah celebration reads Rabbi Salkin's book."
— *Rabbi Harold S. Kushner, author of* When Bad Things Happen to Good People

6" x 9", 224 pp. Quality Paperback, ISBN 1-879045-59-1 **$16.95** HC, ISBN -58-3 **$24.95**

ar/Bat Mitzvah Basics: A Practical Family Guide to Coming of Age Together
dited by Cantor Helen Leneman; Foreword by Rabbi Jeffrey K. Salkin; Intro. by abbi Julie Gordon

6" x 9", 240 pp, Quality Paperback, ISBN 1-879045-54-0 **$16.95** HC, ISBN 51-6 **$24.95**

LIFECYCLES
V. 1: Jewish Women on Life Passages & Personal Milestones
Edited and with introductions by *Rabbi Debra Orenstein*
V. 2: Jewish Women on Biblical Themes in Contemporary Life
Edited and with introductions by
Rabbi Debra Orenstein and *Rabbi Jane Rachel Litman*

This unique three-volume collaboration brings together over one hundred women writers, rabbis, and scholars to create the first comprehensive work on Jewish life cycle that fully includes women's perspectives.

"Nothing is missing from this marvelous collection. You will turn to it for rituals and inspiration, prayer and poetry, comfort and community. *Lifecycles* is a gift to the Jewish woman in America."
—*Letty Cottin Pogrebin, author of* Deborah, Golda, and Me: Being Female and Jewish in America

. 1: 6 x 9, 480 pp. HC, ISBN 1-879045-14-1, **$24.95**; *V. 2:* 6 x 9, 464 pp. HC, ISBN 1-879045-15-X, **$24.95**

LIFE CYCLE...Other books— The Art of Jewish Living Series for Holiday Observance
by Dr. Ron Wolfson

*anukkah—*7" x 9", 192 pp. Quality Paperback, ISBN 1-879045-97-4 **$16.95**

*he Shabbat Seder—*7" x 9", 272 pp, Quality Paperback, ISBN 1-879045-90-7 **$16.95**; Booklet of essings **$5.00**; Audiocassette of Blessings **$6.00**; Teacher's Guide **$4.95**

*he Passover Seder—*7" x 9", 272 pp, Quality Paperback, ISBN 1-879045-90-7 **$16.95**; Passover orkbook, **$6.95**; Audiocassette of Blessings, **$6.00**; Teacher's Guide, **$4.95**

Life Cycle

MOURNING & MITZVAH
• With over 60 guided exercises •
A Guided Journal for Walking the Mourner's Path Through Grief to Healing
by *Anne Brener, L.C.S.W.;* Foreword by *Rabbi Jack Riemer;* Introduction by *Rabbi William Cutter*

"Fully engaging in mourning means you will be a different person than before yo began." For those who mourn a death, for those who would help them, for thos who face a loss of any kind, Brener teaches us the power and strength available t us in the fully experienced mourning process. Guided writing exercises help stim ulate the processes of both conscious and unconscious healing.

"A stunning book! It offers an exploration in depth of the place where psychology and religious ritual intersect, and the name of that place is Truth."
—*Rabbi Harold Kushner, author of* When Bad Things Happen to Good People

7 1/2" x 9", 288 pp. Quality Paperback Original, ISBN 1-879045-23-0 **$19.95**

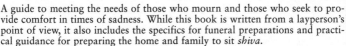

A TIME TO MOURN, A TIME TO COMFORT
A Guide to Jewish Bereavement and Comfort
by *Dr. Ron Wolfson*

A guide to meeting the needs of those who mourn and those who seek to provide comfort in times of sadness. While this book is written from a layperson's point of view, it also includes the specifics for funeral preparations and practical guidance for preparing the home and family to sit *shiva*.

"A sensitive and perceptive guide to Jewish tradition. Both those who mourn and those who comfort will find it a map to accompany them through the whirlwind."
—*Deborah E. Lipstadt, Emory Universit*

7" x 9", 320 pp. Quality Paperback, ISBN 1-879045-96-6 **$16.95**

WHEN A GRANDPARENT DIES
A Kid's Own Remembering Workbook for Dealing with Shiva and the Year Beyond
by *Nechama Liss-Levinson, Ph.D.*

Drawing insights from both psychology and Jewish tradition, this workbook hel children participate in the process of mourning, offering guided exercises, ritua and places to write, draw, list, create and express their feelings.

"Will bring support, guidance, and understanding for countless children, teachers, and health professionals."
—*Rabbi Earl A. Grollman, D.D., author of* Talking about Death

8" x 10", 48 pp. Hardcover, illus., 2-color text, ISBN 1-879045-44-3 **$14.95**

EMBRACING THE COVENANT
Converts to Judaism Talk About Why & How
Edited & with Intros. by Rabbi Allan L. Berkowitz and Patti Moskovitz

A practical and inspirational companion to the conversion process for Jews-by-Choice and their families. It provides highly personal insights from over 50 people who have made this life-changing decision.

"Passionate, thoughtful and deeply felt personal stories....A wonderful resource, sure to light the way for many who choose to follow the same path."
—*Dru Greenwood, MSW, Director, UAHC-CCAR Commission on Reform Jewish Outreach*

6" x 9", 192 pp. Quality Paperback, ISBN 1-879045-50-8 **$15.95**

LIFE CYCLE...Other books
So That Your Values Live On: Ethical Wills & How to Prepare Them
Ed. by Rabbi Jack Riemer & Professor Nathaniel Stampfer

6" x 9", 272 pp. Quality Paperback, ISBN 1-879045-34-6 **$17.95**

Art of Jewish Living Series for Holiday Observance

THE SHABBAT SEDER
by *Dr. Ron Wolfson*

The Shabbat Seder is a concise step-by-step guide designed to teach people the meaning and importance of this weekly celebration, as well as its practices.

Each chapter corresponds to one of ten steps which together comprise the Shabbat dinner ritual, and looks at the *concepts, objects,* and *meanings* behind the specific activity or ritual act. The blessings that accompany the meal are written in both Hebrew and English, and accompanied by English transliteration. Also included are craft projects, recipes, discussion ideas and other creative suggestions for enriching the Shabbat experience.

"A how-to book in the best sense...."
—*Dr. David Lieber, President, University of Judaism, Los Angeles*

7 x 9, 272 pp. Quality Paperback, ISBN 1-879045-90-7 **$16.95**

Also available are these helpful companions to *The Shabbat Seder*:	
•Booklet of the Blessings and Songs	ISBN 1-879045-91-5 $5.00
•Audiocassette of the Blessings	DNO3 $6.00
•Teacher's Guide	ISBN 1-879045-92-3 $4.95

HANUKKAH
by *Dr. Ron Wolfson*
Edited by *Joel Lurie Grishaver*

Designed to help celebrate and enrich the holiday season, *Hanukkah* discusses the holiday's origins, explores the reasons for the Hanukkah candles and customs, and provides everything from recipes to family activities.

There are songs, recipes, useful information on the arts and crafts of Hanukkah, the calendar and its relationship to Christmas time, and games played at Hanukkah. Putting the holiday in a larger, timely context, "December Dilemmas" deals with ways in which a Jewish family can cope with Christmas.

"This book is helpful for the family that strives to induct its members into the spirituality and joys of Jewishness and Judaism...a significant text in the neglected art of Jewish family education."
—*Rabbi Harold M. Schulweis, Cong. Valley Beth Shalom, Encino, CA*

7 x 9, 192 pp. Quality Paperback, ISBN 1-879045-97-4 **$16.95**

THE PASSOVER SEDER
by *Dr. Ron Wolfson*

Explains the concepts behind Passover ritual and ceremony in clear, easy-to-understand language, and offers step-by-step procedures for Passover observance and preparing the home for the holiday.

Easy-to-Follow Format: Using an innovative photo-documentary technique, real families describe in vivid images their own experiences with the Passover holiday. **Easy-to-Read Hebrew Texts:** The Haggadah texts in Hebrew, English, and transliteration are presented in a three-column format designed to help celebrants learn the meaning of the prayers and how to read them. **An Abundance of Useful Information:** A detailed description of how to perform the rituals is included, along with practical questions and answers, and imaginative ideas for Seder celebration.

"A creative 'how-to' for making the Seder a more meaningful experience."
—*Michael Strassfeld, co-author of* The Jewish Catalog

7 x 9, 336 pp. Quality Paperback, ISBN 1-879045-93-1 **$16.95**

Also available are these helpful companions to *The Passover Seder*:	
•Passover Workbook	ISBN 1-879045-94-X $6.95
•Audiocassette of the Blessings	DNO4 $6.00
•Teacher's Guide	ISBN 1-879045-95-8 $4.95

Children's Spirituality

For ages 8 and up   **BUT GOD REMEMBERED**
Stories of Women from Creation to the Promised Land
by *Sandy Eisenberg Sasso*
Full color illustrations by *Bethanne Andersen*

NONSECTARIAN, NONDENOMINATIONAL.

A fascinating collection of four different stories of women only briefly mentioned in biblical tradition and religious texts, but never before explored. Award-winning author Sasso brings to life the intriguing stories of Lilith, Serach, Bityah, and the Daughters of Z, courageous and strong women from ancient tradition. All teach important values through their faith and actions.

•AWARD WINNER•

"Exquisite....a book of beauty, strength and spirituality."
—*Association of Bible Teachers*

9" x 12", 32 pp. Hardcover, Full color illus., ISBN 1-879045-43-5 **$16.95**

IN GOD'S NAME   **For ages 4-8**
by *Sandy Eisenberg Sasso*
Full color illustrations by *Phoebe Stone*

MULTICULTURAL, NONSECTARIAN, NONDENOMINATIONAL.

Like an ancient myth in its poetic text and vibrant illustrations, this modern fable about the search for God's name celebrates the diversity and, at the same time, the unity of all the people of the world. Each seeker claims he or she alone knows the answer. Finally, they come together and learn what God's name really is, sharing the ultimate harmony of belief in one God by people of all faiths, all backgrounds.

•AWARD WINNER•   "I got goose bumps when I read *In God's Name*, its language and illustrations are that moving. This is a book children will love and the whole family will cherish for its beauty and power."
—*Francine Klagsbrun, author of* Mixed Feelings: Love, Hate, Rivalry, and Reconciliation among Brothers and Sisters

"What a lovely, healing book!"
—*Madeleine L'Engle*

| Selected by |
| Parent Council Ltd.™ |

9" x 12", 32 pp. Hardcover, Full color illus., ISBN 1-879045-26-5 **$16.95**

For ages 4-8   **GOD'S PAINTBRUSH**
by *Sandy Eisenberg Sasso*
Full color illustrations by *Annette Compton*

MULTICULTURAL, NONSECTARIAN, NONDENOMINATIONAL.

Invites children of all faiths and backgrounds to encounter God openly in their own lives. Wonderfully interactive, provides questions adult and child can explore together at the end of each episode.

"An excellent way to honor the imaginative breadth and depth of the   •AWARD WINNER•
spiritual life of the young."
—*Dr. Robert Coles, Harvard University*

11" x 8 1/2", 32 pp. Hardcover, Full color illus., ISBN 1-879045-22-2 **$16.95**

Also Available!
Teacher's Guide: A Guide for Jewish & Christian Educators and Parents
8 1/2" x 11", 32 pp. Paperback, ISBN 1-879045-57-5 **$6.95**

Children's Spirituality

A PRAYER FOR THE EARTH
The Story of Naamah, Noah's Wife

or ages 4-8

by *Sandy Eisenberg Sasso*
Full color illustrations by *Bethanne Andersen*

NONSECTARIAN, NONDENOMINATIONAL.

his new story, based on an ancient text, opens readers' religious imaginations
new ideas about the well-known story of the Flood. When God tells Noah
bring the animals of the world onto the ark, God *also* calls on Naamah,
Noah's wife, to save each plant on Earth. *A Prayer for the Earth* describes
Naamah's wisdom and love for the natural harmony of the earth, and inspires
readers to use their own courage, creativity and faith to carry out Naamah's
ork today.

•AWARD WINNER•

"A lovely tale....Children of all ages should be drawn to this parable for our times."
—*Tomie dePaola, artist/author of books for children*

9" x 12", 32 pp. Hardcover, Full color illus., ISBN 1-879045-60-5 **$16.95**

THE 11TH COMMANDMENT
Wisdom from Our Children

For all ages

by The Children of America

MULTICULTURAL, NONSECTARIAN, NONDENOMINATIONAL.

"If there were an Eleventh Commandment, what would it be?"

Children of many religious denominations across America answer this question—
in their own drawings and words—in *The 11th Commandment*. This full-color
collection of "Eleventh Commandments" reveals kids' ideas about how people
should respond to God.

"Wonderful....This unusual book provides both food for thought and insight
into the hopes and fears of today's young."
—*American Library Association's* Booklist

8" x 10", 48 pp. Hardcover, Full color illus., ISBN 1-879045-46-X **$16.95**

SHARING BLESSINGS
Children's Stories for Exploring the Spirit
of the Jewish Holidays

For ages 6-10

by *Rahel Musleah* and *Rabbi Michael Klayman*
Full color illustrations by *Mary O'Keefe Young*

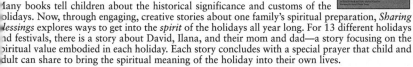

What is the spiritual message of each of the Jewish holidays?
How do we teach it to our children?

Many books tell children about the historical significance and customs of the
olidays. Now, through engaging, creative stories about one family's spiritual preparation, *Sharing
Blessings* explores ways to get into the *spirit* of the holidays all year long. For 13 different holidays
nd festivals, there is a story about David, Ilana, and their mom and dad—a story focusing on the
piritual value embodied in each holiday. Each story concludes with a special prayer that child and
dult can share to bring the spiritual meaning of the holiday into their own lives.

A beguiling introduction to important Jewish values by way of the holidays."
—*Rabbi Harold Kushner, author of* When Bad Things Happen
to Good People *and* How Good Do We Have to Be?

7" x 10", 64 pp. Hardcover, Full color illus., ISBN 1-879045-71-0 **$18.95**

AVAILABLE FROM BETTER BOOKSTORES.
TRY YOUR BOOKSTORE FIRST.

Order Information

# of Copies	Book Title / ISBN (Last 3 digits)	$ Amount
_____	_____	_____
_____	_____	_____
_____	_____	_____
_____	_____	_____
_____	_____	_____
_____	_____	_____
_____	_____	_____
_____	_____	_____
_____	_____	_____
_____	_____	_____
_____	_____	_____
_____	_____	_____
_____	_____	_____
_____	_____	_____

For s/h, add $3.50 for the first book, $2.00 each add'l book
(to a max of $15.00)   **$ S/H** _____

TOTAL _____

Check enclosed for $_____ *payable to:* JEWISH LIGHTS Publishing

Charge my credit card: ❒ MasterCard   ❒ Visa

Credit Card #_____Expires _____

Signature _____Phone (_____)_____

Your Name _____

Street_____

City / State / Zip _____

Ship To:

Name _____

Street_____

City / State / Zip _____

Phone, fax or mail to: **JEWISH LIGHTS Publishing**
P.O. Box 237 • Sunset Farm Offices, Route 4 • Woodstock, Vermont 05091
Tel (802) 457-4000   Fax (802) 457-4004   www.jewishlights.com
Credit card orders **(800) 962-4544** (9AM–5PM ET Monday–Friday)
Generous discounts on quantity orders. SATISFACTION GUARANTEED. Prices subject to change.